SALLY
RIDE

Tam O'Shaughnessy

SALLY RIDE

A Photobiography of America's Pioneering Woman in Space

ROARING BROOK PRESS
New York

Copyright © 2015 by Tam O'Shaughnessy
Published by Roaring Brook Press
Roaring Brook Press is a division of Holtzbrinck Publishing Holdings
Limited Partnership
175 Fifth Avenue, New York, New York 10010
mackids.com

Library of Congress Cataloging-in-Publication Data
O'Shaughnessy, Tam E., author.
    Sally Ride : a photobiography of America's pioneering woman in space / Tam
    O'Shaughnessy. — First edition.
        pages cm
    Summary: "A biography of the famous astronaut drawing on personal and
family photographs from her childhood, school days, college, life in the
astronaut corps, and afterward."— Provided by publisher.
    Audience: Ages 10–14
    ISBN 978-1-59643-994-8 (hardcover)
    1. Ride, Sally—Juvenile literature. 2. Ride, Sally—Pictorial
works—Juvenile literature. 3. Women astronauts—United States—Biography—
Juvenile literature. 4. Women astronauts—United States—Pictorial works—
Juvenile literature. 5. Astronauts—United States—Biography—Juvenile literature.
6. Astronauts—United States—Pictorial works—Juvenile literature. I. Title.

TL789.85.R53O84 2015
629.450092—dc23
[B]
                                                        2015004913

Roaring Brook Press books may be purchased for business or promotional use.
For information on bulk purchases please contact Macmillan Corporate
and Premium Sales Department at (800) 221-7945 x5442 or by email at
specialmarkets@macmillan.com.

First edition 2015
Book design by Roberta Pressel
Printed in China by Toppan Leefung Printing Ltd.,
Dongguan City, Guangdong Province
10 9 8 7 6 5 4 3 2 1

This book is dedicated to Sally,
who inspired us all and
shone brighter than any star.

PROLOGUE

I remember the first time I met Sally. It was a warm summer day at the public tennis courts in Redlands, California. I was twelve years old, standing with dozens of other young tennis players, impatiently waiting to check in at the tournament desk for my first-round match.

As I shuffled forward, my tennis racket hanging from one hand, I noticed a girl with long, sun-bleached brown hair ahead of me in line. She caught my eye because she was standing on her toes. And when she moved forward . . . she walked on her toes like a ballet dancer, but one wearing rumpled white socks and well-worn tennis shoes.

When the girl turned her head, I recognized her. It was Sally Ride. I'd seen her around the other tournaments before, but I'd never spoken to her. Sally saw me staring at her—probably grinning like a frog—and said, "Hi there. Do you know who you play?"

I rolled my eyes and said, "Yes. I play Kris Kemmer. It's the third time I've had to play her this year!"

Sally smiled knowingly and bobbed her head up and down. "Good luck," she said.

Then it was her turn to check in and go play her match. "Good luck," I called out after her.

I had no idea that this brief conversation was the start of a friendship that would last a lifetime, and so much more. This is the story of Sally Ride's life and my part in it.

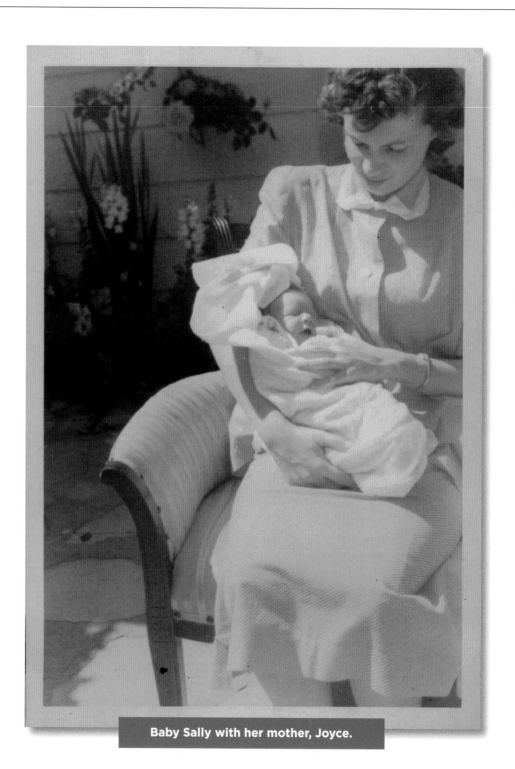

Baby Sally with her mother, Joyce.

No!

SALLY was born in Los Angeles, California, on May 26, 1951.

She grew up in a traditional family. Her father went to work each morning. Her mother stayed home and took care of Sally and her younger sister. The whole family went to church on Sundays.

Baby Sally with her dad.

Sally's father, Dale, was friendly and outgoing. He usually had a smile on his face. He had lots of friends. Dale was a social studies teacher at Santa Monica Junior High School and later a political science professor at Santa Monica City College. He was a sports nut. Dale played racquetball after work and tennis on weekends. He watched sports on TV—everything from tennis and track to basketball and football. Dale loved to play with his girls in the backyard. He made sure they learned how to swim and ride a bicycle.

Dale, Sally, and Joyce on the front lawn of Dale's parents' home in Santa Monica, California.

Sally, two and a half years old, with Dale and baby sister Bear.

Dale taught Sally to ride a bike; Joyce taught her to read.

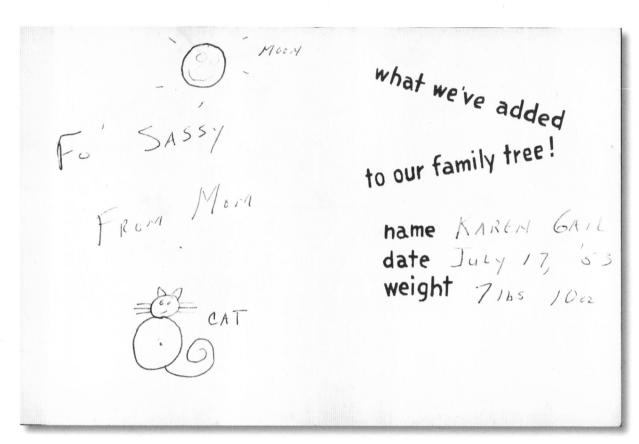

To SASSY
From Mom

MOON

CAT

what we've added
to our family tree!

name KAREN GAIL
date July 17, '53
weight 7 lbs 10 oz

Sally's mom sent her a copy of little sister Karen's birth announcement. Sally called herself Sassy before she could correctly pronounce her name.

Sally's mother, Joyce, was friendly but not as outgoing as her husband. She had a few close friends. Her natural expression was relaxed but thoughtful. Joyce loved to read and think about politics, women's issues, and social causes, and she had a wicked wit. She was active in the Presbyterian Church. She also visited women in prison and helped them stay in touch with their families. Joyce made sure her girls learned how to read and write.

Sally's mother did most of the cooking, but her father pitched in on weekends and when there was company. Everyone shared in cleaning the house and taking care of the yard. Sally and her sister were expected to do their homework and get good grades in school. Other than that, there were few rules. Dale and Joyce were easygoing parents who created a loving, stable home.

Before Sally could say her own name, she called herself Sassy.

When her sister was born, Sally was two years old. She couldn't say Karen. She called her little sister Pear or Perry. Later this changed to Bear. Bear stuck.

She called her little sister Pear or Perry. Later this changed to Bear. Bear stuck.

Sally as a toddler.

Sally and Bear were very different, but got along well. Bear was a naturally kind child. Sally seldom went out of her way for other people. Bear had a wide circle of friends. Sally had one or two close friends. On weekends, Bear often invited one of her friends to spend the night at the Ride home. Sally rarely did this—she liked to spend time by herself, reading or solving puzzles or watching her favorite TV shows *I Love Lucy* and *The Twilight Zone*.

Bear's very first word: **Ta tu (thank you!)**
Sally's very first word: **No (no!)**

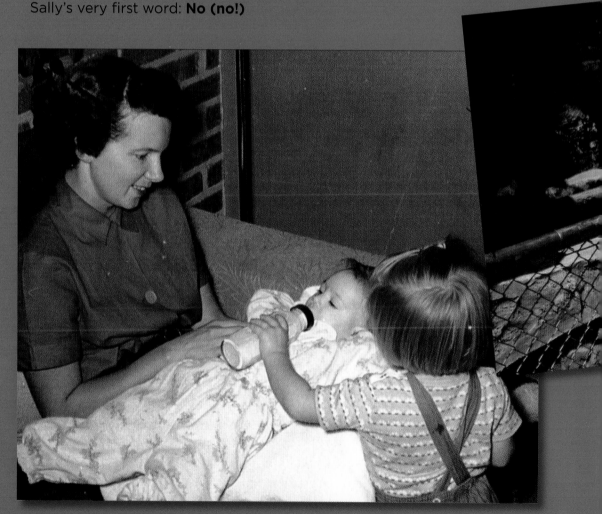

Sally bonded with her baby sister immediately.

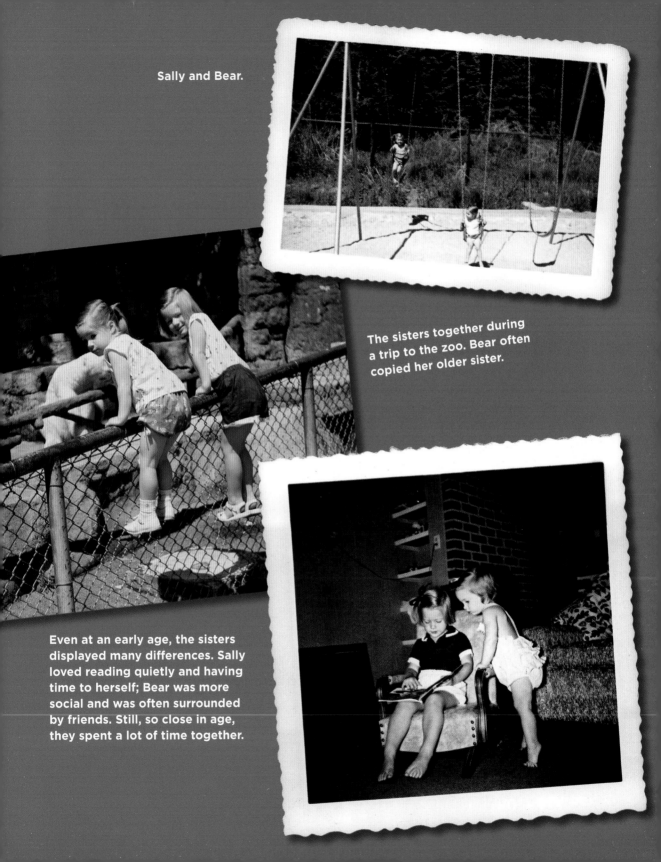

Sally and Bear.

The sisters together during a trip to the zoo. Bear often copied her older sister.

Even at an early age, the sisters displayed many differences. Sally loved reading quietly and having time to herself; Bear was more social and was often surrounded by friends. Still, so close in age, they spent a lot of time together.

Sally and Bear collect pinecones while on vacation.
The girls spent much of their time outdoors.

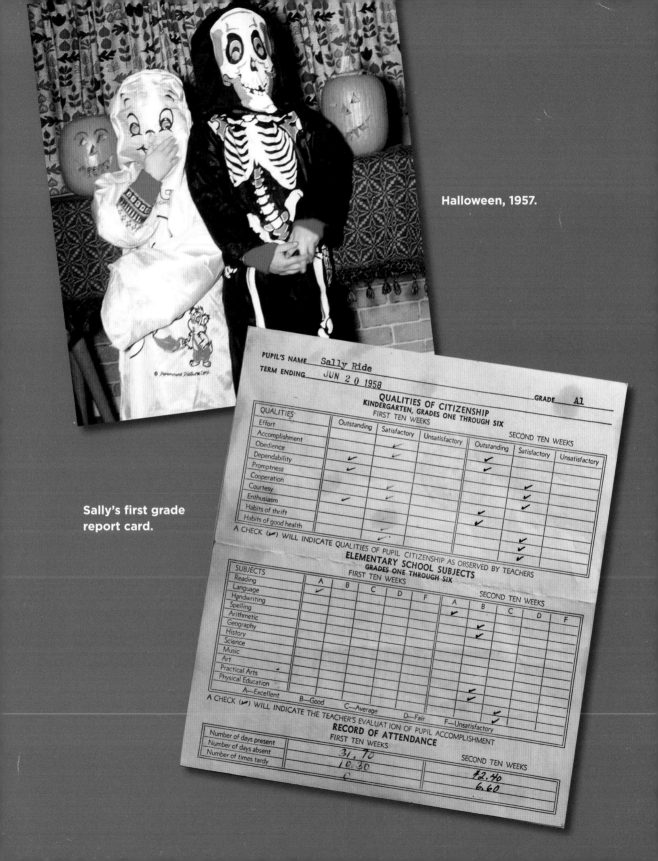

Halloween, 1957.

Sally's first grade report card.

Sally and Bear with their maternal grandmother, Ada.

Both sets of grandparents lived close by. The Ride family spent lots of time with them, but especially with Joyce's parents, Grandma Ada and Grandpa Andy.

Sally's Grandpa Andy taught her how to play baseball. He bought Sally a baseball glove and played catch with her. He sawed off a baseball bat and showed her how to hit. He threw pitches to Sally for hours in the backyard.

Sally listened to Dodger baseball games on the radio with her father and grandfather. After Sally learned to read, she started collecting Dodger players' baseball cards. Her grandfather taught her how to keep track of a game on a scorecard. Her father showed Sally how to read the newspaper box scores.

Sally learned the batting averages of every Dodger player. She memorized the earned run averages of every Dodger pitcher. One of her favorite players was Maury Wills, the great Dodger shortstop from 1959 to 1966. Sally would look up the stats in the newspaper and say, "Grandpa, Maury Wills has 63 hits, and he has batted 242 times this year."

Her grandfather would sit with his arm around Sally and say, "Okay, now divide at bats by hits."

"Grandpa! Maury Wills' batting average is 260!" Sally dreamed of playing shortstop for the Dodgers.

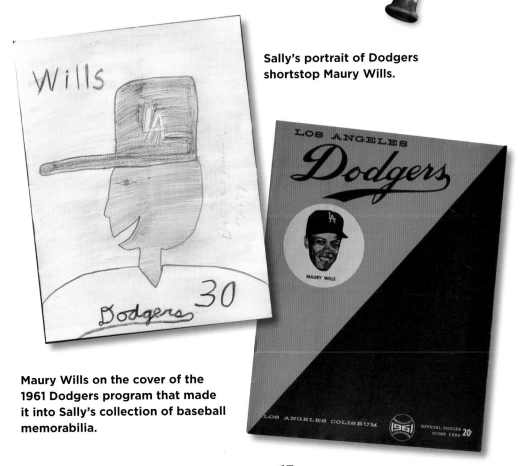

Sally's first baseball bat, sawed off for her by her grandfather.

Sally's portrait of Dodgers shortstop Maury Wills.

Maury Wills on the cover of the 1961 Dodgers program that made it into Sally's collection of baseball memorabilia.

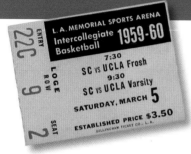

Sally called her father Daddy her whole life. When Sally was a little girl, she went everywhere with him. On weekends they would go to his office at Santa Monica City College. Sally would read in a chair while her father worked at his desk. Sometimes after school, Sally and her father went down onto the field to watch UCLA football practice. Sally's father earned this privilege because he helped student-athletes transfer from Santa Monica City College to UCLA. While Sally's father talked with some of the players and coaches, Sally soaked up the game. They attended UCLA track meets and UCLA basketball home games. Now and then, Dale invited one of the basketball players over for dinner. Sally would open the front door and there might be six-foot-eight-inch Sydney Wicks smiling down at her. Joyce might prepare a big salad and tuna casserole. Everyone sat around the dining room table eating and talking.

Sally was close to her father throughout her life and called him Daddy even as an adult.

For several summers, the Ride family would drive to the San Bernardino Mountains on vacation. They'd rent a cabin by Lake Gregory, where Sally and Bear learned how to fish, water ski, and row a boat.

The Ride family took annual vacations to Lake Gregory.

Sally fishing at Lake Gregory, 1957.

In 1960, when Sally was nine, the Ride family decided to spend a year in Europe. Dale took a one-year sabbatical from Santa Monica City College. The Rides sold their house and furniture in Van Nuys and banked the money for when they returned home.

Spending a year in Europe meant that Sally would miss fourth grade and Bear would miss second grade. Dale and Joyce thought they would learn plenty from their travels. The principal of the girls' elementary school agreed. Visiting different countries, learning about different cultures, and eating different foods would be great learning experiences.

Dale and Joyce planned the trip. They put a world map on a wall in the breakfast room. Sally and Bear traced their trip with a black marker. They stuck pins in the cities they would visit: Amsterdam, Paris, Barcelona, Rome, London, Frankfurt, Copenhagen, and Oslo.

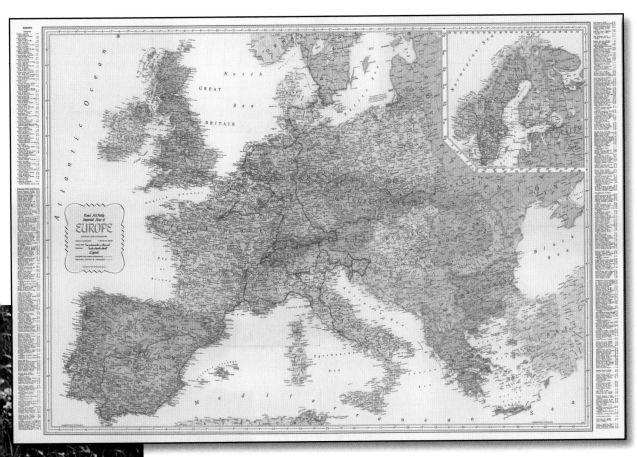

Sally and Bear outlined the family's planned route through
Europe in black marker on this map, which hung in their
breakfast room.

Joyce, Bear, and Sally at the time of their trip to Europe.

In the summer of 1960, the Ride family flew to New York City and boarded a ship called the SS *Rotterdam* for the trip across the Atlantic Ocean. The ship was like a floating neighborhood. Sally and Bear made friends with the other kids. They ran up and down the narrow metal stairs leading to the open-air decks. They raced around and around the hardwood decks. They snuck into every nook and cranny looking for adventure. On the top deck, they played Ping-Pong and a new game, shuffleboard.

Sally and Bear learned to play shuffleboard to pass the time on the ship.

The Ride family poses for a formal photo aboard the SS *Rotterdam*.

The Ride family's receipt for passage to Europe on the SS *Rotterdam*.

Sally and her sister dressed for dinner on the ship.

Dinner was a problem. Sally and Bear had to wash up and wear dresses. They sat at elegant tables with fine china and linens. They ate unfamiliar dishes like supreme of halibut mousseline, creamed endives, and compote with pears. "Where are the hamburgers?" Bear and Sally whispered to each other.

The *Rotterdam*'s menu included fancy cuisines. Sally and Bear craved familiar foods such as macaroni and cheese.

After ten days at sea, the ship docked in the Port of Rotterdam, Netherlands. Joyce and the girls stayed with friends while Dale took a train to Bremen, Germany, to pick up their new station wagon, a Borgward. They named their new car Borgy.

Sally, Joyce, and Bear inside Borgy, the car the family purchased in Europe.

Bear and Sally in Lucerne, Switzerland.

Hiking up a snow-covered hill in Serfaus, Austria.

Atop a wall in Vienna, Austria.

Scraping snow off Borgy.

Bear, Joyce, and Sally with their Aunt Karen and Uncle Lars in Norway.

The Ride family drove all over Europe in Borgy. They visited museums and historic places, they saw friends in France and Italy, and they stayed with relatives in England and Norway. In Norway, Uncle Lars taught them how to snow ski. In Copenhagen, they bought Danish teak furniture.

When the family visited St. Mark's Square in Venice, Sally put a huge handful of seeds in the hood of Bear's jacket. Dozens of pigeons landed on Bear's head and back. Sally started calling her little sister "Pigeonhead."

The girls sprinkled birdseed onto the ground and into their hoods. Dozens of pigeons swarmed to eat.

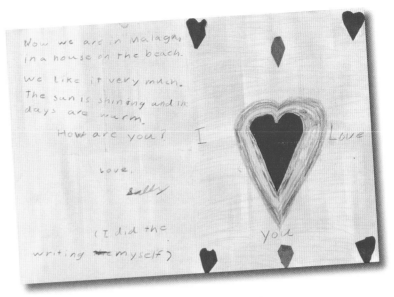

Now we are in Malaga, in a house on the beach.

We like it very much. The sun is shining and the days are warm.

How are you?   I   Love

love,

Sally

(I did the writing ~~me~~ myself)

you

As the Ride family drove from place to place in Europe, Sally was the navigator. Her mother showed her how to read a map. Her father taught her how to use the math formula: distance = speed x time. He explained to Sally that if she knew two of the three numbers, she could figure out the missing number. Sally loved knowing this. She would find the distance on the map, from, say, Malaga to Barcelona, Spain, carefully write down the formula, and do the math to find how long it would take the family to reach their destination.

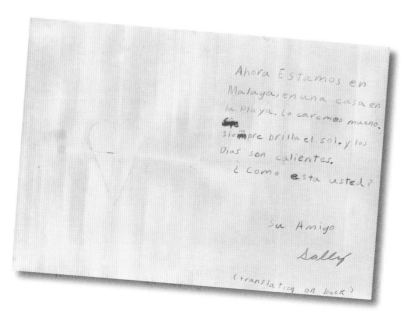

Ahora Estamos en Malaga, en una casa en la Playa. Lo caremos mucho. Siempre brilla el sol, y los Dias son calientes.
¿Como esta usted?

Su Amigo

Sally

(translation on back)

On this card sent home to her Grandma Ada and Grandpa Andy, Sally wrote her message in both Spanish (left), and English (above).

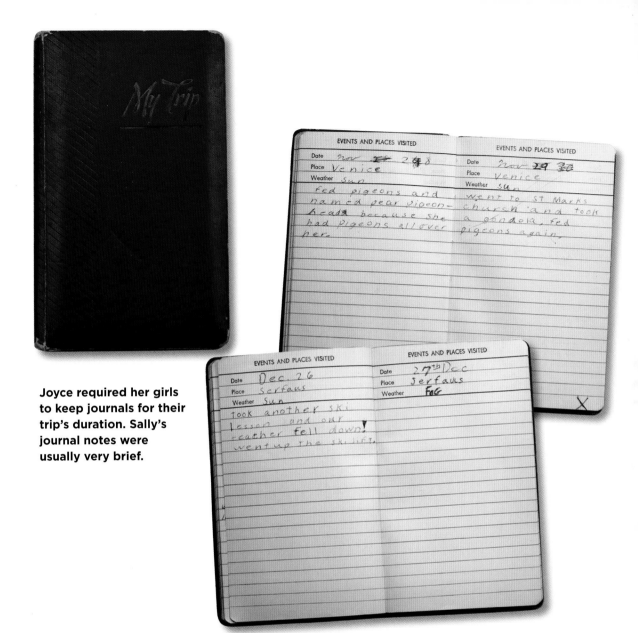

Joyce required her girls to keep journals for their trip's duration. Sally's journal notes were usually very brief.

Still, Sally was desperate to get Dodger baseball scores. Her grandfather would mail them to her from time to time.

Sally's mother wanted the girls to keep journals about their adventures in Europe, but they were too busy having fun to write very much. This did not go unnoticed by Joyce. She suggested that Sally and Bear start stamp collections. Everywhere they went the family bought stamps. Sally collected Olympic stamps. Bear collected stamps of animals.

SS *Rotterdam*.

After almost a year away from home, the Ride family drove back to Amsterdam and boarded the SS *Rotterdam* for their long trip home. They shipped Borgy and their new teak furniture back to California with them.

Borgy's license plate.

Sally's father's passport, covered in dozens of stamps from the countries the family visited.

Sally serving.

2

I swear on a stack of tennis rackets . . .

In the spring of 1961, the Ride family returned home from Europe. They bought a ranch-style house on a cul-de-sac in Encino, California—a suburb of Los Angeles in the San Fernando Valley east of the Santa Monica Mountains. They furnished it with their new Danish teak chairs, tables, couches, and lamps. Joyce planted rose bushes in a sunny patch of the front yard. Orange trees and lemon trees lined the lawn next to the fence in the backyard. Dale drove Borgy to work. That fall, Bear began third grade and Sally started sixth grade at a new school. Sally skipped fifth grade because she tested ahead of her age group in reading and math.

One February day during sixth grade, Sally's science teacher wheeled one of the school's black-and-white TV sets into the classroom to see astronaut John Glenn blast into space from Cape Canaveral, Florida. Launch minus 10 seconds . . . 9 . . . 8 . . . 7 . . . The computers checked the rocket engine. 3 . . . 2 . . . 1 . . . The rocket lit! Blastoff! The rocket leaped off the launch pad in a trail of fire. Clouds of steam billowed behind. The class watched as John Glenn became the first person to go into orbit around our planet. After the launch, Sally noticed that she was clenching her fists. Her hands were clammy. Sally wiped her hands down the front of her skirt and then slid her desk back to its usual place.

Sally's parents gave her a chemistry set so she could do simple experiments, and bought a subscription to *Scientific American* magazine. Sally would read it from cover to cover. She would stare at the illustrations for hours.

Sally's first microscope, 1963.

Later in sixth grade, Sally made a model of an atom out of Styrofoam balls and wire. When she was done she couldn't stop staring at her atom. Sally was amazed by what her teacher had told the class: "Atoms are so tiny we can't see them with our eyes. But everything in the universe is made out of atoms—the moon and stars, but also you and me, mountains and trees, houses and cars." Sally was fascinated. She tried to make sense of what she was learning . . . the universe is too large to imagine; atoms are too little to see. Sally felt on fire to learn more.

One weekend, Joyce steered the Borgward into the garage and called out to Sally and Bear, "Come help me with the groceries."

When the girls walked into the garage—surprise! There was a collie cowering in a corner. Shortly after the family moved into their new home, Joyce saw an ad in the newspaper—collie needs home. She called the telephone number in the ad and arranged to pick up the one-year-old dog.

"Come here little girl," Sally said gently to the frightened dog. Bear and Sally urged the collie into the house with treats.

Grandma Ada and Grandpa Andy sit on the couch while Sally and Bear play on the floor with the family dog, Tsigane.

Tsigane checks out a TV dinner tray.

Because *Lassie* was a popular TV show at the time, Bear wanted to name their new dog Lassie. Sally didn't like the idea. Joyce reminded the girls of Tsigo, a dog they played with in Europe. At an inn in the former Yugoslavia, they saw a family throwing snowballs to a black Labrador retriever named Tsigo. He would race after the snowballs, catch them in his mouth, and then gently carry them back intact. Sally and Bear were thrilled with this trick and joined in the game. The sisters agreed to name their new dog Tsigane, the feminine form of Tsigo, which means gypsy.

In the backyard, goofing around with Tsigane.

Sally loved to play sports. She loved to move. On warm summer days she played baseball at the end of the street with the boys on the block. She played golf with her Grandpa Andy on the course behind her grandparents' house. Sally loved to run, skip, and jump. She loved to throw a baseball, catch a football, and swing a golf club.

One day, Sally was playing catch with some girls on the playground at school. A group of boys watched. One of the boys walked over to Sally and snickered, "Girls aren't supposed to throw a ball the way you do. What a tomboy!"

"I'm not a tomboy! I'm a girl!" Sally replied. Her feelings were hurt. She didn't understand why the boy was being mean to her—just because she could throw a ball well. Sally was used to the boys in her neighborhood. They liked it that she was a good athlete; they picked her for their teams.

Although Sally wasn't very tall or strong, she had nimble hands, quick feet, and an analytical mind. These made her a good athlete.

When Sally was about ten years old, her mother showed her how to play tennis. Soon Sally was playing junior tennis tournaments almost every weekend. She was speedy around the court. When Sally's opponent hit a ball too short, Sally liked to return it deep, race to the net, and then smack a volley for a winner.

The Ride family went to church every Sunday. Once Sally started playing tennis, though, she was allowed to stop going. Instead, Sally's father drove her to tennis tournaments all over Southern California— from Santa Barbara to San Diego. He loved to watch her play and talk with the other tennis parents. Sally could tell when her father was nervous watching her play a close match. He would cross one leg over the other and just about shake his foot off.

Joyce and Bear kept going to church. Like her mother, Bear loved being involved in church activities—from listening to sermons to going to socials to doing community work.

Sally practicing her serve.

Sally's tennis racket, 1964.

In the summer of 1962, Sally took her first tennis lessons. They were small group lessons with a few other girls and boys. Sally also took a few private tennis lessons from Alice Marble, the famous tennis champion of the 1930s. No one knows exactly what happened, but for some reason Alice and Sally rubbed each other the wrong way. Many years later in a newspaper article, Alice said of Sally, "She had a lot of athletic ability. But she seemed so frustrated by it. She would hit me with the tennis ball. I had to duck like crazy. It wasn't that she mis-hit the ball. She had perfect aim. She was doing it."

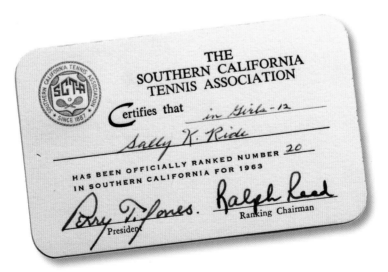

Sally's Southern California Tennis Association card. She was officially ranked number 20 in Girls 12 and Under in Southern California in 1963.

Bear, Sally, and tennis champion Alice Marble. Sally's dislike for her teacher is evident on her face.

Sally loved to read her whole life.

As Sally grew up, she discovered that she loved science. She loved to know things.

Moonlight is really sunlight bouncing off the moon's surface.

Atoms are made of protons, neutrons, and electrons.

The strongest muscle in the body is the tongue.

Sally's parents bought her a small telescope. In the evening, she would set it on a table in the backyard and look at the moon. Sally saw the craters in the lunar highlands and the dark splotches of frozen lava called lunar maria. She wondered, *What would it be like to stand on the moon?*

When it was completely dark, Sally would look up at the night sky without her telescope. There was Venus below the crescent moon. There was Jupiter higher up in the sky. And there was Orion, her favorite constellation. With a big grin on her face, she would trace the twinkling stars in Orion's belt with her finger and then go back inside the house to do her homework.

Sally's first telescope, a gift from her parents.

Sally's teachers liked it that she was a smart girl. But maybe more, they liked it that she was eager to learn. When a natural interest or an inspiring teacher motivated Sally, she would study like crazy. The more she knew, the more she wanted to learn.

Sally (center, wearing a white dress and yellow belt) at middle school graduation.

Sally with her tennis pal, Whitney Grant.

Sally played doubles in tennis with Whitney Grant. Sally and Whitney were not cutthroat competitors like some of the other girls and boys on the junior tennis circuit. They enjoyed the competition, but they were easygoing about the outcome. Whitney and Sally came up with their own hand signals. Together they made manuals and bound them with pink ribbon. On the last page of the manuals they wrote:

I swear on a stack of tennis rackets to keep our hand signals a secret. If I break this promise, I will eat this book!

—————————— Whitney Grant

—————————— Sally Ride

Sally and Whitney playing doubles.

Sally at the net.

46

In the summer of 1965, Whitney's father suggested to Dale that Sally apply to the elite Westlake School for Girls. Whitney went to school there, and Mr. Grant was recruiting for the high school tennis team. Westlake was a private school with a good reputation, and only fifteen students in each class. Sally applied to Westlake and received a half scholarship to play on the tennis team. Dale taught civics at Westlake to pay for the rest of Sally's tuition in trade, on top of his community college teaching job. He later did the same thing for Bear.

Above: Sally's tenth grade picture.

Left: Sally and Dale, dressed for Westlake's tenth-grade dance.

Bear later followed in Sally's footsteps and enrolled at Westlake.

Sally lays up during a basketball game.

Sally's Westlake basketball team. Sally is second and Whitney is seventh from the left.

The Westlake tennis team. Pictured along with Sally (front row, kneeling on right) and her teammates are tennis greats Pancho Segura, Dennis Ralston (standing, first and second from left), Rod Laver, Westlake Tennis Coach Constantin Tanasescu, and Fred Stolle (standing, fifth, sixth, and seventh from left).

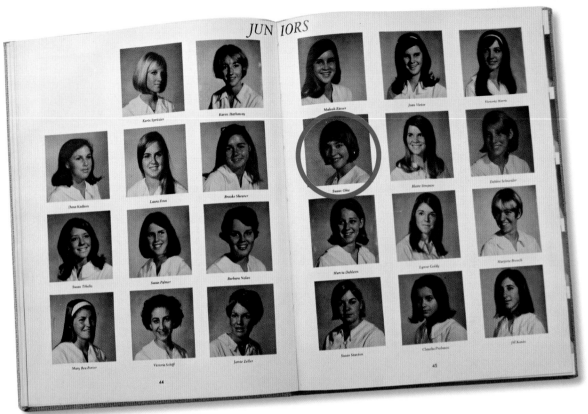

Sally's best friend in high school was Sue Okie, pictured here on the right page.

Sally's best friend in high school was Sue Okie. They both had scholarships and carpooled together, one hour from the San Fernando Valley where they lived, to their school in Beverly Hills. Both Sue and Sally felt a little out of place among some of their classmates—the daughters of famous actors and wealthy business tycoons. The friends both liked science and were in most of the same classes together.

Sally didn't have much patience for English class. When her eleventh-grade English teacher, Miss Bredlow, said something that Sally thought was silly, she would look at Sue and smirk. At least once her teacher caught Sally with that expression on her face and yelled at her. Sally wasn't flustered. Then during twelfth grade, Sally and Sue had Mrs. Schulmeister for English. She also gave a weekly seminar in the evening for a select group of students, including Sue and Sally. In seminar, the students read Sartre's *Nausea* and Camus' *The Plague*. Sally didn't say much in class or seminar, but she and Sue thought their teacher was brilliant. They also thought that—unlike Miss Bredlow—she was a little scary. One time, Mrs. Schulmeister caught Sally smirking or rolling her eyes or not putting in much effort in class, and she publicly humiliated her. "Sally, I see that our discussion of Ovid is of no interest to you. Please tell us why the poet's early life and transformation from privileged child to epic poet bores you," Mrs. Schulmeister said with icy disapproval. Sally was horrified—everyone was staring at her! No one spoke or moved; the classroom was dead silent. Sally tried to control herself, but she couldn't. She burst out of her desk chair and ran out of class. Sue followed her. She found Sally standing in the hall with her head down, trying hard not to cry. Sue had never seen Sally so upset.

Sally's junior yearbook. She is pictured in the lower right-hand corner.

When Sally started Westlake in tenth grade, it was only the second year the all girls' school offered science courses as part of the curriculum. It was the first year that trigonometry and calculus were taught. People were just starting to realize that girls liked, and excelled in, science and math just as boys did.

In eleventh grade, Sally took physiology. Her teacher was a Hungarian woman named Dr. Elizabeth Mommaerts. She had been a researcher, with her husband, in the department of physiology at UCLA. Dr. Mommaerts was an inspirational teacher. She used a college physiology textbook, and she challenged her students to *really* learn how the human body works. She gave enthusiastic, crystal-clear lectures on the heart, the lungs, the brain, and the other organs and how they work together. The culminating project for the course was the dissection of a fetal pig. Sally and her lab partner named their pig Sir Frances Bacon.

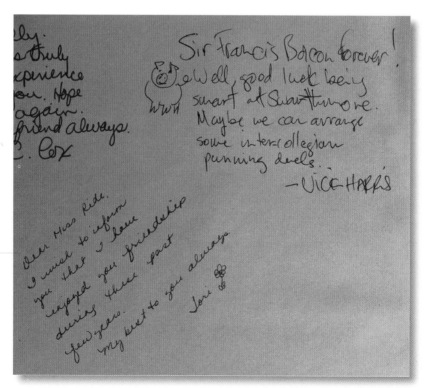

An entry by Sally's lab partner in her yearbook commemorates the fetal pig they dissected together, whom they dubbed Sir Francis Bacon.

Dr. Elizabeth Mommaerts taught physiology and was Sally's favorite high school teacher.

Dr. Mommaerts's signature in Sally's 1967 Westlake yearbook.

all good things
to Sally one of
my dear dear juniors
Mo. Mommaerts

Some of Sally's Westlake report cards.

Report Card 1

WESTLAKE SCHOOL

The grades of RIDE, Sally
for the quarter ending 4/7/67

	Quar.	Exam.	SEM.
English III	B-		
Mathematics Algebra II	B		
History United States	A		
Language Spanish II	A-		
Science Physiology	A		
Art History			
Art			
Choral			
Music Appreciation			
Commercial			
Other			
Physical Education	A		
Deportment	S+		
Absence	2		
Times Tardy	0		

A-excellent   D - passing
B - good   F - failing
C - average

Report Card 2

WESTLAKE SCHOOL

The grades of RIDE, Sally
for the semester ending 6/16/67

	Quar.	Exam.	SEM.
English III	B	B-	B
Mathematics Alg. II	B	A	B+
History U.S.	B	89	B+
Language Span II	A-	A-	A-
Science Physiology	A	A	A
Art History			
Art			
Choral			
Music Appreciation			
Commercial			
Other			
Physical Education	A		A
Deportment	S+		S+
Absence	3		5
Times Tardy	0		0

A-excellent   D - passing
B - good   F - failing
C - average

Report Card 3

WESTLAKE SCHOOL

The grades of Sally RIDE
for the quarter ending 11/10/67

	Quar.	Exam.	SEM.
English IV	B+		
Mathematics IV	B+		
History			
Language Spanish III	A-		
Science Chemistry	A-		
Art History			
Art			
Choral			
Music Appreciation			
Commercial			
Other			
Physical Education	B+		
Deportment			
Absence	0		
Times Tardy	0		

A-excellent   D - passing
B - good   F - failing
C - average

Before and After · · ·

UCLA
High School Honors Program

...ide, Louise Steinman, Pat Mittry, Debbie
Gwen Field, Toni Turner, Brooke Shearer.

Sue Okie, Dana Kadison (absent), Maleah Eisner,
Francine Applebaum.

*here we
are again
but is so much...*

ninety-one

**Sally and her classmates
never tired of having fun.
Sally is lying down in front,
and Sue is in the middle with
her chin resting on her hands.**

Sometimes Dr. Mommaerts would go off on tangents about life, careers, puberty, and motherhood. The girls in her class loved to listen to her talk about these things.

Dr. Mommaerts's exams were tough. Sally didn't always study hard enough for them. Sometimes she studied in the car on the way to school! Once Sally came to class unprepared for a test on the kidney. One of the questions was: Draw and label a nephron. Sally didn't have a clue what a nephron looked like or how it worked, so she made up something. She drew a large circle with lots of little circles inside it. Dr. Mommaerts was outraged. She gave Sally a hard time and wouldn't let her forget it.

Dr. Mommaerts spent extra time mentoring students, especially Sally and Sue. She talked with them after school and in between classes through eleventh and twelfth grades. She gave them brainteasers and science puzzles to do. She encouraged Sue and Sally to stick with science. She challenged Sally to take a college course during her senior year. Sally took Physics for Poets at UCLA. By the end of her senior year, Sally would decide to major in physics at college.

The summer before Sally's senior year of high school, her parents decided to let her drive the family's Rambler to school. They even let her get the old car painted. Sally would pick up Sue and take Mulholland Drive along the Santa Monica Mountains to school. Simon and Garfunkel, the Beatles, or Diana Ross and the Supremes would be blaring from the car radio. Sally would proudly park the banana yellow Rambler in the Westlake parking lot right next to the other students' brand-new sports cars— Porsches, Mustangs, and Pontiac GTOs.

Underachiever!

That's what Sally's friends called her in high school. When Sally wasn't interested in something, she wouldn't give it her all. Her classmates knew she could ace a paper or an exam if she wanted to. But sometimes Sally was content just to get by.

Dear Sally-

I'll always remember your "fatal" and "not so fatal" shots—Keep up your tennis! "Gross underachieving!" If you don't drop me a postcard once in a while—I'll really kill you! Good luck.
Love always J.
(alias Bonnie or Clyde)

Sally,

To the most wonderful underachiever I know—
I hope to be hearing lots of news about what you're *not* doing. Seriously, have a great year full of many tennis balls and free time.
Love, M.

Throughout high school, Sally competed on the junior tennis circuit. One of her best friends was Ann Lebedeff. When Ann wrote a letter or card she signed it

40-love!
Ann-the-Pro.

Sally thought this was funny. So she started signing her letters

40-love!
Sally

The Lebedeff family lived near San Diego. The Lebedeff home was a hub for tennis because they had a tennis court in their backyard. Ann's parents and her sisters Geni, Kathy, and Joanie played tennis. Sometimes Sally would take the train from Los Angeles to Carlsbad to practice with Ann.

Sally during a break on the Lebedeffs' tennis court.

The Lebedeff sisters and dog Bingo, Tam (middle), and Tam's sister Kim. Sally took the photo.

Ann Lebedeff and Tam were doubles finalists in the 1968 National Girls' 18 and Under Championships.

Ann and I were doubles partners and good friends. Sometimes when Sally was visiting Ann, I would be there, too. Ann, Sally, and I would get out a big basket of tennis balls, fill tennis ball cans with water to drink, and do our favorite tennis drill—two-on-one. Ann would play alone on one side of the court against Sally and me on the other side of the court. The goal was to keep the ball in play. Sally and I would make Ann run like crazy all over the court, hitting ball after ball after ball. Then we'd switch and Sally or I would take a turn and try to last longer.

After practice, Ann, Sally, and I would go hiking with Ann's sisters and dog Bingo through the orange groves and up the hill to the lake. Mrs. Lebedeff would make tacos or spaghetti and lay out mounds of food for dinner. Afterward Ann and Sally and I and Ann's sisters would play records and dance in the den. At first Sally would hang back and hope no one would notice her. But sooner or later one of us, usually me, would take her hand and pull her into the middle of the room, and she would slowly loosen up and dance with the rest of us.

When tennis tournaments were in Los Angeles, Ann and I would go over to the Rides' house. Sally, Ann, and I would take turns playing each other at Ping-Pong in the den. In between matches we'd eat Baskin-Robbins ice cream. Tsigane always got a lick of ice cream, too. On the record player, the Who, the Rolling Stones, or the Beatles played.

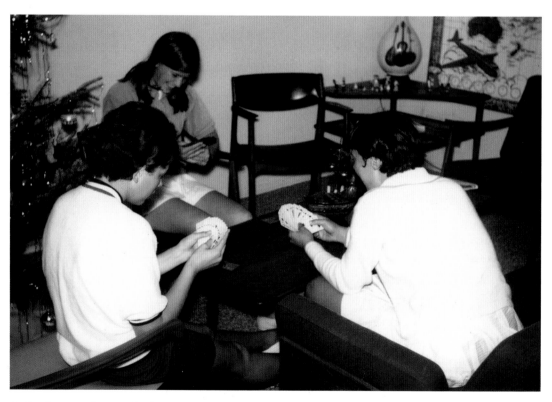

Sally, Ann, and Tam playing cards at the Ride home during a tennis tournament in December 1967. Sally is smiling, so she probably won the hand!

Above: Contestants at the 1968 National Girls' 18 and Under Championships. Sally and Whitney Grant are next to each other in the second row (sixth and seventh from the left). Ann Lebedeff and Tam are in the front row (seventh and twelfth from the left). Right: Sally kept a program from the 1968 USLTA Girls' 18 and Under National Championships.

51st ANNUAL
**USLTA Girls' 18
National Championships**
on the Grass Courts of the
PHILADELPHIA CRICKET CLUB
August 12th to 17th, 1968

Each summer, Sally traveled to the east coast to compete in national junior tennis tournaments. So did Ann, Whitney, and I. Kentucky, Missouri, Illinois, Ohio, Pennsylvania, Delaware, and New York are very different from California. They are hot and humid in the summer. Tennis is played on slow clay courts or fast grass courts. We missed the predictable ball bounces of the hard courts we grew up on in California. And almost every afternoon, it rained cats and dogs as thunderstorms blew through. When Sally was playing a match and saw dark clouds rolling across the sky, she got ready to run. If she saw a bolt of lightning, Sally started counting. One one-thousand, two one-thousand, three one-thousand . . . Boom! Light travels faster than sound. So when

Sally and her Westlake teammates won their school's first invitational tennis tournament in a very close competition.

The Winner—Westlake By Half A Point!

Westlake School's tennis pro, Constantin Tanasescu, host for the school's first invitational tournament, chats with Cindy Crosby, Mayfield; Sally Ride, Westlake, and Patty Hogan, Bishop's School, La Jolla, who won the team singles. Eavesdropping are two Westlake fathers (from left), Dale Ride and Kurt Mann, who watched contestants from 19 private girls' schools play matches Saturday and Sunday, Oct. 29 and 30.

you see lightning, count the number of seconds before you hear thunder. That will tell you how far away the storm is. The fewer seconds you count, the closer the storm. She learned the trick from her eighth-grade science teacher.

Back in California, Westlake held a college fair one evening on campus. Sally talked with Fred Hargadon, the dean of admissions at Swarthmore College in Pennsylvania. Swarthmore was very near where Sally played the Girls' 18 and Under National Championships with Ann, Whitney, and me.

Sally and Dean Hargadon walked outside, and Sally pointed out all the planets and constellations she could see. They talked about tennis. Sally's father had graduated from Haverford College near Philadelphia, so he was familiar with Swarthmore College. And when Sue was accepted into Swarthmore, Sally decided to go there, too. She would play number one on the women's tennis team. She would study physics.

Sally was off to college.

Sally (standing, right) was playing a tennis tournament in Delaware during the historic *Apollo* lunar landing on July 20, 1969. She stayed up late to watch Neil Armstrong become the first person to walk on the moon. The next day, she won her first-round match.

Sally receives her diploma at Westlake's graduation.

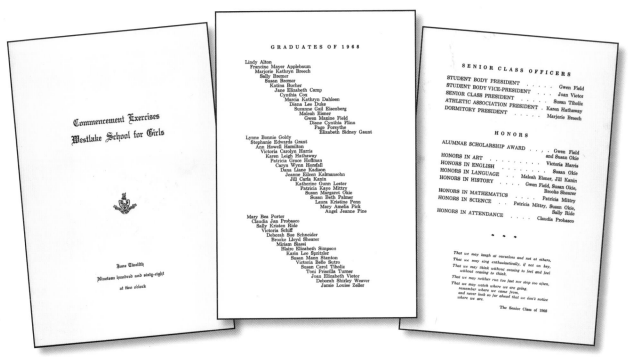

Westlake's graduation program.

The Ride family in 1968.

3

Physics explains everything!

In the late summer of 1968, Sally's whole family drove cross-country from California to Pennsylvania to drop her off at college, stopping along the way at places like the Grand Canyon National Park. They helped Sally move into her dormitory room. Then Joyce, Dale, and Bear said goodbye to Sally and headed home.

LOST?

A framed cartoon given to Sally by her father when she left for Swarthmore.

Wilson
OFFICIAL

TENNIS SCORE CARD

ROUND	BEST OF	SETS
FINALS	EVENT WOMEN'S EASTERN COLLEGIATE	

SALLY RIDE **VERSUS** PAT GARCIA
Swarthmore   MARY BALDWIN

WON BY *Sally Ride*

SCORE 6-3 6-4

COURT NO.   DATE *Oct. 12, 1969*

UMPIRE *Lee Jackson*

For more Sets of better and faster play, specify

WILSON *Championship* **TENNIS BALLS**

WILSON SPORTING GOODS CO.

CHICAGO · NEW YORK · AND OTHER LEADING CITIES

© 1940 WILSON SPORTING GOODS CO.   AV 300

Sally's winning scorecard from the Eastern Collegiate Tournament.

At Swarthmore, Sally played on the women's basketball and field hockey teams. She played number one on the women's tennis team. During their freshman year, she and Sue Okie spent time together in and out of classes, and Sally went out with the placekicker on the football team. Within her first few months, she declared physics her major.

The Times SLANT on Youth
DELAWARE COUNTY (PA.) DAILY TIMES, FRIDAY, NOV. 21, 1969   PAGE 20

SALLY RIDE, a sophomore at Swarthmore College is the number one woman college tennis player in the East.

AT SWARTHMORE COLLEGE

Tennis, Astrophysics Keep Miss Ride Busy

A newspaper article featuring Sally's win in the Eastern Collegiate Tournament.

Winner In Eastern Collegiate Tournament

Miss Sally Ride of Swarthmore College was the singles winner in the Eastern Collegiate Tennis Tournament played at State University College at New Paltz, defeating Miss Pat Garcia of Mary Baldwin College, Virginia in straight sets, 6-3, 6-4. Miss Ride was seeded first and Miss Garcia third.

There were 128 women participants from 36 colleges who played in the tournament last weekend.

Jill Eisman and Diana Parker defeated Talbert Jordan and Mary Tomkins in the doubles finals, 6-3, 6-2. Both doubles teams were from Mary Baldwin College and the second seeded team defeated the first seeded team.

Miss Margaret Lutze, associate professor of physical education at State University College at New Paltz, made the tournament arrangements.

Local newspapers recognized Sally as extraordinary, both academically and athletically.

Before too long, though, Sally started feeling homesick. She missed California. Pennsylvania gets lots and lots of snow in the winter, so tennis is played indoors. Also, the competition wasn't as good as it was in California. So, after one and a half years at Swarthmore, Sally called her parents and told them she wanted to come home. She also sprang the news on Sue, who was completely surprised: she had no clue that Sally was homesick! But this was nothing new. Even as a teenager, Sally was closed-mouthed about her feelings. It was just the way she was—she didn't talk about personal things very much. Sue was sorry to see Sally leave. She would miss her brainy, athletic best friend.

Sally's summer 1970 UCLA registration card.

Sally loved Swarthmore, but missed home. She eventually transferred to Stanford to be closer to her family—and Tsigane, of course!

Something else was on Sally's mind, too. She wondered if she could make tennis her career.

As a junior tennis player, Sally couldn't make herself practice as often or as long as some of her friends did. She realized that this was her chance to find out if she could be a disciplined athlete. So the summer after she came home from Swarthmore, Sally devoted herself to tennis. Meanwhile, to keep up her studies, she took courses on quantum mechanics and Shakespeare at UCLA.

Sally worked hard on her tennis every day. Her goal was to improve enough to be able to return one more shot during points. This doesn't sound like a lot, but Sally knew it would help her beat some of the players above of her in the rankings. With her practice partners, Sally hit forehands and backhands crosscourt and down the line in long rallies. She hit hundreds of volleys and tens of overheads. She loved to volley—it was her favorite shot. With her fast feet and quick reactions, Sally was all over the net. Her good hands let her carve short volleys or punch deep ones. Sally practiced her serve, hitting basket after basket of balls to each side of the court and to different spots in the service box. Her hard work paid off! Sally's fitness, footwork, and ball control improved.

Sally running down a forehand in a tennis match during the Pacific Southwest Tennis Tournament held at the Los Angeles Tennis Club.

In the summer of 1972, Sally taught tennis at TennisAmerica in Lake Tahoe, California, where she played an exhibition doubles match with tennis legend Billie Jean King. After the match, Billie Jean told Sally that if she worked hard enough, she could someday play on the pro tour. Though Sally was flattered by the compliment, she knew better.

In Sally's physics lab at UCLA, her teaching assistant was a young man named John Tompkins. He was a few years older than Sally and in graduate school studying physics. Sally and John started spending time together outside of class. They talked about physics. They went to UCLA football games together. John drove Sally to tennis tournaments and watched her play.

Sally kept working on her tennis game. But after several months of hard work, she finally had to admit to herself that she wasn't cut out for professional tennis. Sally didn't enjoy practicing. She realized that she didn't have the physical discipline to be a professional athlete. She was disappointed. But as a college student, first at Swarthmore and now taking courses at UCLA, Sally knew she loved to learn. She loved physics, and she recognized that she had the mental discipline to be a physicist!

Sally on the Stanford campus.

As luck would have it, Fred Hargadon, the dean of admissions at Swarthmore College, had accepted a similar job at Stanford University in California. He had stayed in touch with Sally's father. He recruited Sally to play on the Stanford women's tennis team and made sure she received a transfer application. The admissions committee reviewed Sally's application and liked what they saw—she had made good grades in math and physics courses—and admitted her to the then mostly male physics department. At the end of the summer in 1970, Sally packed her books, clothes, and tennis gear. She drove her old red Toyota Corona to Palo Alto, near San Francisco, to start her junior year at Stanford University. In the meantime, John flew to Russia to continue his physics research. Sally and John promised to stay in touch and to see each other whenever they could.

At Stanford Sally worked part-time to help her parents pay for her tuition, dormitory room, and books. Sally's first job was in the registrar's office. This gave her access to student records. Even though she wasn't supposed to, Sally searched the computer records to see if she knew anyone in her class. When she got to the *T*s, she saw a familiar name, Tyson, Molly. Molly! Sally thought.

Each year, the Westlake School for Girls tennis team had played the team from Marlborough School, where Molly went to high school. Sally didn't know Molly very well, but at least she knew someone at Stanford! Sally looked up Molly's address. When she got home from her job and classes, Sally grabbed her tennis racket and some tennis balls and walked across campus to find Molly's dorm. When Molly opened the door, Sally said, "Hi, there. You're the only person I know at Stanford. Want to go hit some tennis balls?"

Sally and Molly hit it off. They started spending lots of time together. They met for breakfast in the student cafeteria. They practiced with the tennis team in the afternoon after classes. Sally played number one singles and Molly played number six singles on the team. Their coach wanted Sally to play doubles with the number two player on the team. Sally said, "No, I want to play doubles with Molly." And she did.

The men's tennis team played their matches on courts in the middle of campus near the athletic department. The men's courts were kept in perfect condition. They had bleachers for fans to sit and watch the matches. The women played on rundown tennis courts, with weeds growing through cracks. They were on the edge of campus, with no place for spectators to sit.

"This isn't fair!" Sally told Molly. Her friends on the men's team had tennis scholarships that paid for most of their school expenses. The guys also had money for tennis clothes, tournament entry fees, and travel to compete against other schools. There were no women's athletic scholarships at Stanford. At that time, none existed at any college, anywhere in the country. So the women's tennis team had no money—zero. Sally and the other players on the women's tennis team paid for everything with their own money.

Sally and Molly drove together in Sally's car to play against other women's college tennis teams in Northern California. On long road trips, Sally and Molly would memorize scenes and speeches from Shakespeare's plays. Sally had taken a course on Shakespeare at UCLA and liked it. Molly was studying Shakespeare as part of her English major. Sally decided to major in both physics and English. Sally's high school friends from Westlake couldn't believe it . . . Sally? English?

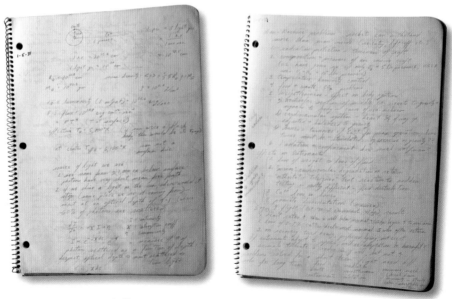

Sally's notes from a physics seminar.

Typing a college paper.

When Sally walked into her physics classes, she would sit down next to mostly men. There were only four women among the twenty-four physics majors in her graduating class. When Sally sat down in her English classes, she was surrounded by other young women. Nearly half of the 179 English majors in her graduating class were women.

When Sally was a teenager, she would tell people she was going to be an astrophysicist when she grew up. She said that mostly because she liked to surprise people. But once Sally actually started studying physics, she loved it. "Physics explains everything!" she would say to her friends. Sally liked that physics explains how the whole universe works—from the Big Bang 13.8 billion years ago to now; from subatomic particles, atoms, and molecules to stars, solar systems, and galaxies; and from a barren rocky planet 4.6 billion years ago to a lush green Earth loaded with living things that float, swim, crawl, wiggle, walk, run, and fly.

Sally got good grades in school, but she wasn't obsessed with getting straight *A*s. She made her fair share of *A*s, but she got plenty of *B*s, too. Sally got a *C* in one of her physics courses—Electricity and Magnetism. She couldn't stand the subject. "No one really understands electricity and magnetism!" she would say with a sneer. Sometimes Sally would rather play volleyball, or hit tennis balls, or watch her favorite soap opera—*All My Children*—than study.

After almost a year away in Russia, John Tompkins came home for a visit. Sally and John had exchanged long letters with each other. They saw each other several times that summer before John returned to Russia and Sally went back to school.

Then at the beginning of Sally's senior year, she got a letter from John saying that he was breaking up with her. He hoped they would stay friends. Sally was hurt. Molly comforted her. In that moment, Sally realized she was in love with Molly. And Molly felt the same way. Sally didn't have a clue what it meant. Sally just knew she wanted to spend every second with Molly.

At that time, society viewed being gay as wrong. So deep down, Sally felt ashamed and afraid. What would happen if someone found out? Sally kept her feelings to herself, and Sally and Molly kept their relationship a secret.

Back at school, Sally and Molly started playing volleyball with some of the guys in Sally's physics class. This became a regular fun thing to do—everyone just showed up at the volleyball courts and played for hours.

As time passed, tension built up between Molly and Sally. Molly wanted to be more open about their relationship. Sally thought it was nobody's business. She had her friends in the physics department and she had Molly. That was enough for Sally.

Molly could no longer stand the secrecy. She was tired of pretending. After graduation, Molly broke up with Sally. Sally was heartbroken.

Molly Tyson, Sally, and Molly's brother, Ben.

Sally working with a telescope at Stanford.

Dale, Sally, and Joyce at Sally's Stanford graduation.

Sally's diploma in physics.

Sally stayed on at Stanford to continue studying physics as a graduate student. Molly took a job as a sports writer and eventually moved to New York City.

Sally had always kept her emotions hidden. So she went to class, she did her physics research, she played volleyball with her friends, and she pretended everything was fine. But Sally missed Molly.

Sally walked around with a heavy heart. She dug into her physics studies. She started seeing one of her physics classmates, Bill Colson, on and off. They talked about physics. They ran 10K races on weekends. Sometimes after a race, they would go out for breakfast. Sally always ordered the same thing—waffles with vanilla ice cream.

Sally gets ready to pass the volleyball to Bill Colson, a fellow physics graduate student whom she occasionally dated.

Then Ann Lebedeff moved to the San Francisco Bay area and a few months later I did, too. After high school, Sally, Ann, and I had scattered in different directions. Like Sally, Ann started college and competed on the women's tennis team. I delayed going to college and played professional tennis on the Women's Tennis Association tour. Now we were back together. Sally was happy to have us around. Ann and Sally joined a rugby team. Sally and I learned how to play platform tennis and played doubles together in a few tournaments. Some mornings, the three of us played tennis before going to work; some weekends, we ran in the hills behind the Stanford campus. We laughed about our junior tennis days and talked about our plans for the future.

Sally (right) and Ann Lebedeff joined a rugby team in Palo Alto.

Playing rugby. Sally running in the dark shirt (center right).

Then we scattered again. Ann became the women's tennis coach at the University of Arizona and moved to Tucson. I left my job as publisher of the Women's Tennis Association newsletter and moved to Atlanta, Georgia, to study biology.

Sally was sorry to see us go, but she was nearing the end of her physics research. After seven years at Stanford, she was about to finish writing her dissertation on free-electron lasers—lasers that create a beam of light by sending clumps of electrons through magnetic fields. Most of this work is theoretical—Sally sat at her desk with a bunch of pencils and a stack of paper. She spent hours lost in thought, working through equations. These complex calculations let Sally imagine—like a cartoon running through her head—what electrons would do if they passed through a magnetic field in outer space. Once Sally's dissertation was finished, she would present her findings to her three mentors, the physics professors on her committee. If they liked what they read and heard, Sally would earn her Ph.D. in physics. Dr. Sally Ride!

Sally planned on becoming a university professor. She liked teaching, doing research, and the university life. But one day while Sally was eating scrambled eggs and a cinnamon roll in the student cafeteria, she glanced at the student newspaper and something caught her eye—NASA to recruit women. NASA was recruiting astronauts, and for the first time women could apply.

A Stanford student newspaper article reporting that, for the first time, NASA was recruiting women for the astronaut training program.

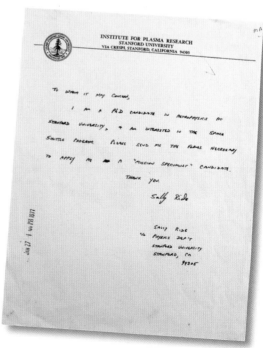

Sally's note to NASA requesting an application to the astronaut program.

Sally's essay explaining why she wanted to join the astronaut corps, part of her application to NASA. "Now that the space program has evolved to the point where astronauts are being selected from the scientific community, and women are being considered, I feel that I'm being offered an incredible opportunity."

Up until then, most astronauts had been military pilots—and they were all men. That's because people didn't think a woman could handle a job like being an astronaut. But the women's movement—the struggle for equal legal, economic, and social rights—was changing ideas about what women could do. Now NASA was looking for scientists and engineers and encouraging women to apply.

Sally's stomach tingled. Her heart raced. All of a sudden, Sally realized that she wanted to be an astronaut. She hurried back to her house and wrote a letter to NASA requesting an application.

When Sally told her parents that she had applied to become an astronaut, they thought, *Sure, why not?* Joyce and Dale didn't think her chances of getting picked were very good. But then they thought again. *Hmm . . . Sally is a scientist. She is an athlete. She is cool as a cucumber under pressure. Maybe Sally has an excellent chance!*

A few weeks later, Sally received an application from NASA. She sent it in and then received a longer application. This one requested her medical history and asked her to write an essay about why she wanted to be an astronaut. A few months later, Sally received a telegram from NASA inviting her for an interview. In August 1977, Sally flew to NASA's Lyndon B. Johnson Space Center in Houston, Texas. She was there for a week. The NASA selection committee interviewed her. She attended briefing after briefing and dinner after dinner, with medical exams and psychological assessments in between.

Back at Stanford, Sally tried not to think too much about NASA and becoming an astronaut. Instead, she focused on finishing her dissertation.

Then early one morning, Sally was awakened by a phone call from George Abbey, the Johnson Space Center's director of flight operations. He said, "We've got a job here for you, if you're still interested in taking it." Sally had made the cut. She was going to be an astronaut! Sally wondered if she was dreaming—it was five o'clock in the morning. She waited as long as she could and then called her parents.

Sally called Sue, too. "Hi. This is your friendly local astronaut," she said. Sally's voice told Sue everything she needed to know.

Postcard from NASA confirming receipt of Sally's application, and the telegram congratulating Sally on her acceptance into the astronaut corps.

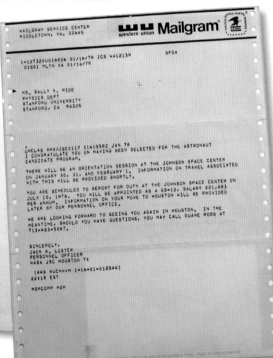

Sally relaxes after a run at The Dish, Stanford University's radio telescope.

Sally wished she could call her high school science teacher, Dr. Mommaerts. But six years after Sally and Sue graduated from high school, Dr. Mommaerts had committed suicide. Before her death, she had gone through some rough times. She had rejected all the things she loved, including teaching and science. Her death was a crushing blow to Sue and Sally. Sally told Sue, "She's the one person in the world I wanted most to call—even more than my parents. And I can't."

When NASA announced the new class of astronauts—with six women, the first female astronauts to join the U.S. space program—the media went crazy. The physics department was bombarded with telephone calls from reporters all over the world. On the day of the announcement, Stanford arranged a press conference for Sally. The room was packed with newspaper and television crews and lots of cameras—the lights blinded Sally. Hundreds of TV, newspaper, and magazine stories were written. Sally wasn't used to all the attention . . . she was a physicist, not a movie star.

And she still had to finish her Ph.D. When she read the last sentence of her dissertation, Sally sat back and smiled. *I'm done!* Then something dawned on her. Sally realized that she knew something that no one else in the whole world knew yet—the results of her research. She liked the feeling a lot. *This is the coolest thing about being a scientist,* Sally thought to herself.

NASA's timing was perfect. Sally successfully defended her dissertation, got into her green VW Rabbit, and drove to Houston.

Number of applications NASA received: 8,079
Number of applications from women: 1,251
Number of finalists: 208
Number of women finalists: 21
Number chosen to become astronauts: 35
Number of women chosen: 6

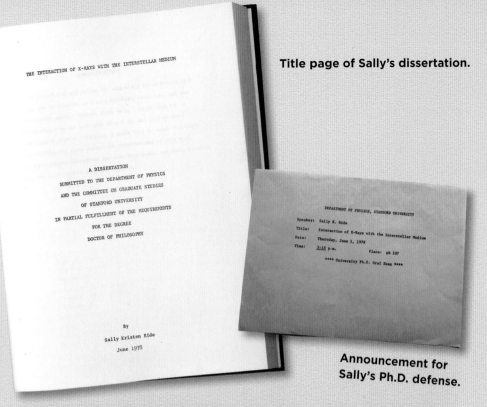

Title page of Sally's dissertation.

Announcement for Sally's Ph.D. defense.

Sally's Stanford Ph.D. diploma.

Sally's "casual" photo for NASA, 1978.

4

What do astronauts do?

In the summer of 1978, Sally started astronaut training at the Johnson Space Center (JSC for short) in Houston. Her class included five other women—NASA's first female astronauts—and twenty-nine men. They called themselves the thirty-five new guys, or the TFNGs. Sally had no idea what to expect. *What do astronauts do?* she wondered.

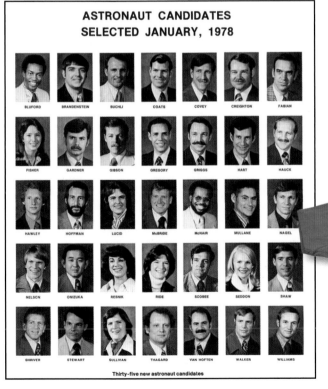

**ASTRONAUT CANDIDATES
SELECTED JANUARY, 1978**

BLUFORD — BRANDENSTEIN — BUCHLI — COATS — COVEY — CREIGHTON — FABIAN

FISHER — GARDNER — GIBSON — GREGORY — GRIGGS — HART — HAUCK

HAWLEY — HOFFMAN — LUCID — McBRIDE — McNAIR — MULLANE — NAGEL

NELSON — ONIZUKA — RESNIK — RIDE — SCOBEE — SEDDON — SHAW

SHRIVER — STEWART — SULLIVAN — THAGARD — VAN HOFTEN — WALKER — WILLIAMS

Thirty-five new astronaut candidates

Sally's 1978 NASA astronaut class.

Sally's astronaut class referred to themselves as the thirty-five new guys and made up blue and red shirts branded "TFNGs."

NASA's first female astronauts.

U.S. AIR FORCE T-38A NO-80
A.F. SERIAL NO. 69-7084
SERVICE THIS AIRCRAFT WITH GRADE
JP-4 FUEL. IF NOT AVAILABLE. T.O. NO
42B1-1-14 WILL BE CONSULTED FOR
EMERGENCY ACTION
SUITABLE FOR USE OF AROMATIC FUEL

Sally sitting in one of NASA's T-38 jets.

Sally preparing to board a T-38 jet.

Most of the existing astronauts were former fighter pilots from the air force and navy. But the new recruits were mostly scientists—physicists, medical doctors, astronomers, chemists, oceanographers, and engineers. The brand-new space shuttle was changing the direction of the space program. NASA was focusing more on science and technology. Sally and the others brought new skills and different perspectives, which made the astronaut corps more versatile. This was important because when astronauts are in space, they might be asked to capture a damaged satellite, study the effects of weightlessness on a salamander, or fix a broken air filter.

A WOMAN'S PLACE IS IN THE COCKPIT!

The staff at JSC—around 4,000 engineers and scientists—was almost all male.

That meant NASA had to make a few changes before the female astronauts arrived. They added a women's locker room to the astronaut gym. They bought hair dryers, tampons, and makeup.

At first the thirty-five rookies trained together. They were fitted for flight suits and helmets. They learned how to fly NASA's sleek, white T-38 jets. They learned how to eject and operate a parachute just in case there was trouble. Flying these swift jets makes astronauts think fast. This is good practice for spaceflight. It's dangerous in space. If something unexpected happens, astronauts have to think fast and act quickly.

Sally loved to fly. Her flying partner was usually John Fabian. He was an engineer and air force pilot before becoming an astronaut. John and Sally would fly from Houston over the Gulf of Mexico. John sat up front in the pilot's seat. Sally sat behind him in the copilot's seat. John and Sally would zoom over the ocean at 500 mph. John would pull back the stick, and they would climb straight up. Sally's head and body would be pressed tight against her seat by the pull of 5 Gs, or five times the force of gravity. She couldn't even lift a finger. After not too long, John would start to level off,

Sally snapped these shots from the copilot's seat as John Fabian landed their T-38.

Fellow astronaut Steve Hawley, Dale, Joyce, and Sally.

and Sally would start to relax. Then John would jam the stick to one side and the jet would roll over. John and Sally would be flying upside down . . . over the ocean . . . going 500 mph. "You just don't enjoy this enough," Sally would shriek into her headset.

Sally and the other astronauts liked to wear their aviator sunglasses and leather jackets everywhere. "When we go out for pizza together, we look more like a motorcycle gang than a group of astronauts," Sally said with a grin.

Sally's private pilot's license.

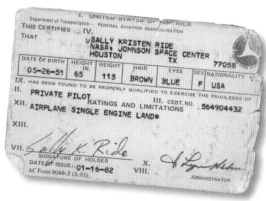

A piece cut from Sally's shirt—a ritual following a pilot's first solo flight.

Bear became an ordained Presbyterian minister the same year Sally became an astronaut.

Trying on each other's professional clothing. The girls never outgrew goofing off together.

Most of astronaut training is like being in school. Sally and the other new astronauts sat in classrooms listening to lectures. Sally listened closely and wrote page after page of notes. She studied all sorts of new subjects—from engineering, radio communications, and navigation to biochemistry, geology, and oceanography. Sally soaked up everything about the space shuttle and its life-support systems. She learned all about spaceflight—from rocket fuels, countdown, liftoff, and escape velocity to weightlessness, orbit, reentry, and landing.

Sally's NASA ID card.

Parachute training.

As part of their training, the astronauts got to act like teenagers again. Yes, they were preparing for spaceflight . . . but they were also having lots of fun. The TFNGs trained in parachute jumping, water survival, scuba diving, and the extreme G-forces of a rocket launch. They learned how to float weightless inside the "vomit comet": a special airplane that is empty inside except for padding on the walls, ceiling, and floor. After the airplane takes off and reaches a certain altitude, it dips and dives, then it climbs and dips and dives again. Each time the plane dives, it simulates the feeling of weightlessness for about 20 seconds. Floating in the plane and doing somersaults in midair is fun. But the dips and dives are like being on a roller coaster—they make some astronauts feel sick to their stomachs. Sally lucked out; she wasn't bothered by the roller coaster ride.

Sally recovers from a session inside NASA's giant centrifuge.

Parachute training.

Water survival drill.

It didn't take long for the TFNGs to become a close-knit group. On weekends, they took turns having barbecues at their homes. They held cooking contests to see who could make the best Texas chili.

Sally did her own training, too. She lifted weights in the astronaut gym, and she ran five miles a day, five days a week. Sally ran in her neighborhood or on the back roads around JSC. Sometimes she had to jump over roadkill—flattened armadillos.

NASA's first six female astronauts (left to right): Sally, Shannon Lucid, Kathy Sullivan, Rhea Seddon, Anna Fisher, and Judy Resnick.

A break during training.

After a year of training, Sally was assigned to work with a team to design the space shuttle's fifty-foot robot arm. She spent two years working on it and little else. Even though this was an engineering job and Sally had been trained as a physicist, she took to it. She was able to imagine how the arm needed to work in space, and she was able to communicate this clearly. Sally's teammates were impressed.

Sally and the five other female astronauts felt extra pressure to prove themselves. They wanted to show NASA—and the world—that women could do as well as men in every situation. Above all, they wanted to get their turn to fly—they wanted to be assigned to a space shuttle crew. The selection of crews was a mystery: no one really knew how these decisions were made. So the six female astronauts didn't have a reason to compete against each other. Each just worked hard and tried her best. Yet, the question on everyone's mind was, *when will I fly?* The other question they couldn't help wondering was, *which one of us will fly first?*

On April 12, 1981, the first space shuttle flight blasted off from the John F. Kennedy Space Center in Florida. *Columbia* carried only two astronauts on its first flight—veteran commander John Young and pilot Bob Crippen. The brief two-day mission was a success! It proved that the shuttle was an exciting and practical new way to get astronauts to space and back. Never before had a spacecraft launched like a rocket, orbited like a spaceship, and landed like an airplane.

For the second and third flights of the space shuttle *Columbia*, which launched in November 1981 and March 1982 in turn, Sally was picked as CAPCOM, or capsule communicator. This is an important job: the CAPCOM relays every message from Mission Control on the ground to the astronauts in space. That meant Sally had to know every little thing about the shuttle— every system, every switch, every drawer and its contents, and how to repair every part.

Sally at Mission Control, working as CAPCOM during shuttle flight STS-2.

It wasn't all work though. Sally selected the wake-up music for the crews. "Pigs in Space" from the Muppets was one of her choices.

Once again Sally got high marks on her work. Commander Bob Crippen, the pilot of the first space shuttle flight, STS-1, noticed. Crip would pilot the seventh flight, and he was getting ready to recommend crewmates. That mission would include one of the six women astronauts—NASA's first female astronaut.

Something happened to Sally while she was training at NASA. All of her knowledge, skills, and experiences came together—her teamwork, her ability to understand the gist of things, her physical coordination, her clear style of communicating, her easygoing way with people. But something else happened, too. For the first time in her life, Sally gave something her all—and she loved it! Sally was completely committed to her work—mind, body, and spirit. In a letter to Sue, Sally wrote, "I have lost my dominant trait, which has been not to work at things. I'm really working hard, and I am enjoying it. In fact, I am obsessed with it."

One morning in April 1982, Sally was called in to see George Abbey, the director of flight operations at JSC. Sally wondered why he wanted to see her. George said, "Uhm, how do you like the job you've got now?"

Sally didn't know what to say because her job as CAPCOM had just ended. She replied, "Well, what is my job?"

George said, "Sally, you are going to fly on the shuttle. You have been assigned to STS-7 under Crip's command."

Sally couldn't believe her ears. *I am going to fly in space!*

Just as the boys on the block in Sally's childhood picked her for their teams, the men in the physics department at

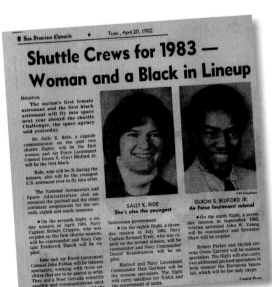

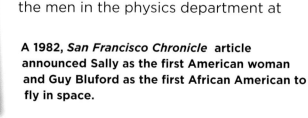

A 1982, *San Francisco Chronicle* article announced Sally as the first American woman and Guy Bluford as the first African American to fly in space.

Newsweek magazine, June 13, 1983.

People magazine, June 20, 1983.

Stanford and now the men at NASA had picked her for their teams, too. All her life, people wanted Sally to be part of their team—because she was competent, determined, and cool under pressure, and because she was truly a team player.

When Sally's selection was announced, it must have been a blow to the other five female astronauts. But it didn't take long for everyone to accept that her turn to fly on the shuttle would come.

Almost overnight, Sally became one of the most famous people in America. She appeared on the covers of *Newsweek*, *Ms.*, and *People* magazines. She was interviewed on every major television news program. When Sally spoke to reporters at a NASA news conference announcing her selection, they asked her some silly questions. It was a shock for some people to think of a woman in a role such as an astronaut.

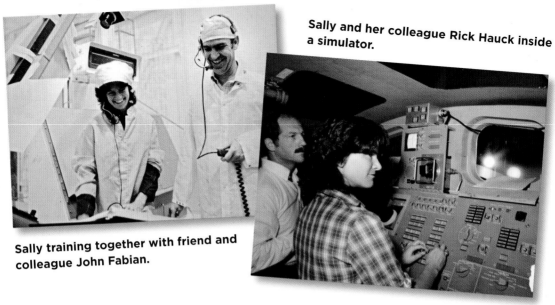

Sally and her colleague Rick Hauck inside a simulator.

Sally training together with friend and colleague John Fabian.

"Do you cry when you are under pressure?"

"Why doesn't anyone ask Rick that question?" Sally wondered out loud.

"Are you going to wear a bra in space?"

"There's no sag in space," Sally replied.

"How will you handle your period in space?"

Glare. No reply.

Sally's friends could tell that she was annoyed with the questions. But one of the reasons NASA leaders chose Sally was that they believed she could handle the pressure of being a celebrity. They were right. Sally politely but briefly answered the reporters' questions. Afterward she added, "It's too bad our society isn't further along and this is such a big deal. It's time we realized that women can do anything they want to."

After all the excitement, Sally was glad to get back to work. She spent the next year training with her four crewmates—Bob Crippen, John Fabian, Rick Hauck, and Norm Thagard. Sally worked long hours with Crip and Rick practicing launch and reentry, and with John and Norm rehearsing with the robot arm in the shuttle simulator—a life-size replica of the shuttle cockpit that mimics the movements and sounds of the real one. In between, Sally stayed up late studying, learning procedures, and stuffing facts into her brain.

Sally got along well with the other astronauts. But she really liked Steve Hawley. Steve was a lanky, redheaded astronomer who grew up in Kansas.

Steve liked Sally a lot, too. They both loved college basketball. Steve grew up in Kansas and was a fan of the University of Kansas Jayhawks. Sally, of course, was a fan of the UCLA Bruins. They played pranks on each other. A Jayhawks decal would suddenly appear on Sally's locker. A Bruins T-shirt would somehow wind up in Steve's gym bag.

In early 1982, Sally called her parents and her sister and told them that she and Steve wanted to get married. Sally asked her sister Bear, who had become a Presbyterian minister, to marry them.

Bear, together with Steve's father, married Sally and fellow astronaut Steve Hawley on July 24, 1982.

Sally and Steve cutting their wedding cake.

12 San Francisco Chronicle ★ Sat., August 14, 1982

Wedding of Astronauts

Houston

Astronaut Sally Ride, set to become the first American woman to fly into space, and astronaut Steve Hawley were married last month in Salina, Kan., the couple confirmed yesterday.

"We didn't want to make a big deal of it," the new Mrs. Hawley told a reporter, "We only told a few friends."

The couple took two days off for the July 24 wedding in the bridegroom's hometown.

Mrs. Hawley, 31, is scheduled to become the first American woman in space as a member of the crew of the seventh space shuttle mission, now set for next April.

Hawley, 30, is an astronomer and has not been selected for a specific space mission.

They were in the same group selected for astronaut training in January of 1978. They are the second astronaut couple to wed. Rhea Seddon and Robert L. Gibson married last year and are the parents of a son.

Associated Press

ASTRONAUTS SALLY RIDE AND STEVE HAWLEY
She is set to be the first American woman to go into space

Steve and Sally's union made national headlines.

The STS-7 pre-launch crew breakfast.

When she was a little girl, Sally liked to sit in the backyard after dinner and watch the sky grow dark as the sun set behind the Santa Monica Mountains. Soon she'd see the first twinkles of light against the blackness of night. Sally would search the sky for Orion. If her favorite constellation was out, she would trace the stars in Orion's belt with her finger.

Just before dawn on the morning before launch, Sally repeated her childhood ritual. This time, though, she gazed up at a dark sky and picked out familiar points of light from a beach in Florida outside the astronauts' crew quarters. The day was June 18, 1983—the day Sally would become the first American woman to fly in space.

Sally's launch-countdown schedule.

BEFORE LAUNCH

As we drove toward the launchpad, the shuttle looked quiet and peaceful. But when we got there and stepped out of the van, I could hear it hissing and crackling as though it were alive.

Besides a crowd of 250,000 around the outskirts of the Kennedy Space Center, 4,000 special guests showed up at Sally's launch, including actors, politicians, women's rights activists, and musicians. Each crewmember is allowed to have fifty friends and family watch his or her launch from a special observation site. A few months earlier, Sally sent out invitations to everyone important in her life. Sally's parents, Joyce and Dale, came. Bear came with her husband, Shannon, and one-year-old son, Whitney. Sally's friends from tennis, Westlake, and Stanford came to watch her blast off into space, including Ann, Whitney, Sue, Molly, Bill, and me.

Geni Lebedeff, Bear, Ann Lebedeff (kneeling), Whitney Grant, and Tam pose in front of Sally's photo at the STS-7 launch party.

Joyce and Dale at the STS-7
launch party.

Dale and Joyce's guest passes from Sally's STS-7 launch.

From launch control, Steve spoke into his headset: "Sally, have a ball!"

LIFTOFF

Once the rockets lit, the shuttle leaped upward in a cloud of steam and a trail of fire. Inside the ride was rough and loud. My head rattled around inside my helmet; my body bounced against my seat. I could barely hear the voices in my headset above the roar of the rockets.

Dale's photos of the STS-7 launch.

Dale watches the STS-7 launch.

One of many messages supporting Sally and her fellow crewmembers.

During launch, Sally couldn't just sit back and enjoy the ride. She had work to do. As rocket fuel exploded beneath her, Sally monitored computer screens, read the checklists, and ticked off milestones. It was exhilarating and terrifying at the same time. If anything went wrong, she was expected to find the correct procedure—and fast! Seven seconds after ignition—when the shuttle starts to roll—Sally said, "Roll program" into her headset, telling Mission Control that the shuttle was on track. Those words were the hardest words Sally ever had to get out of her mouth. It's not easy to speak seven seconds after launch!

ENTERING ORBIT

It feels like your arms are made of lead. The notebook in your lap seems to weigh a ton. Then suddenly, the shuttle engines stop. The lead in your arms vanishes. Your arms are lighter than air, and your notebook floats up in front of your face. You are in space.

Sally loved looking back at Earth from space. Here, she basks in the light streaming in through a window and looks down on her home planet.

Sally, Rick, and Norm brought their TFNGs T-shirts with them to space.

During the mission, Sally was the first astronaut to use the fifty-foot robot arm—which she had helped design—to capture a satellite as it hurtled around Earth. The robot arm works like a human arm. It bends in three places like shoulder, elbow, and wrist joints. Sally thought, *Just because this was easy to do in the simulator, doesn't mean it is going to be easy to do in space!* She wrapped her fingers slowly around the joystick and switched on the arm. *This is real metal that will hit real metal if I miss,* she thought. Sally took a deep breath. Then, with patience and precision, she slowly moved the arm out of the cargo bay. She gently grasped the satellite. She pulled it toward the shuttle and lowered it into the cargo bay for safe storage. The operation came off without a hitch. With a big grin on her face, Sally sighed in relief. She'd proved that the robot arm was an important space tool.

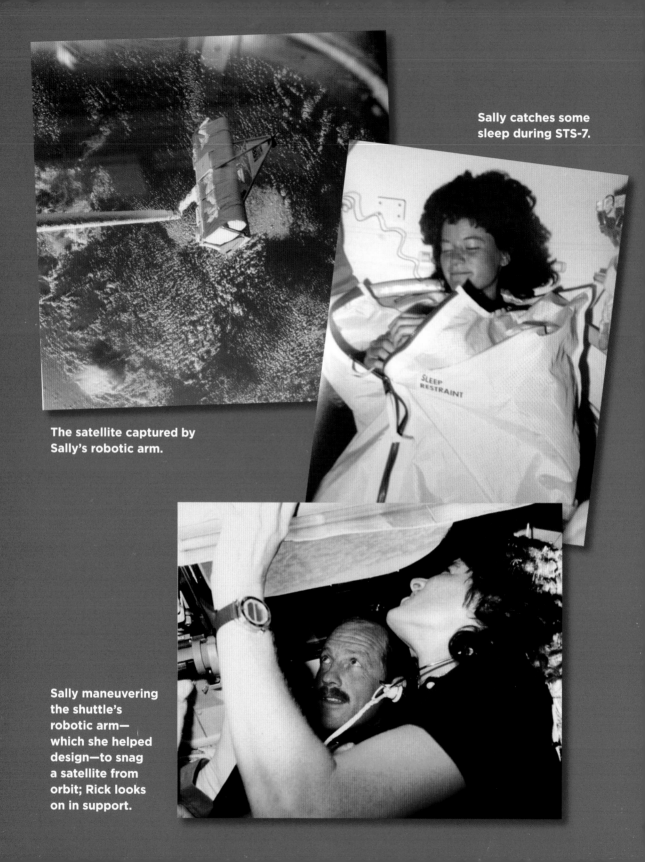

Sally catches some sleep during STS-7.

The satellite captured by Sally's robotic arm.

SLEEP RESTRAINT

Sally maneuvering the shuttle's robotic arm—which she helped design—to snag a satellite from orbit; Rick looks on in support.

A satellite photo of the shuttle. Sally came up with the idea of shaping the arm into a 7 as a tribute to the crew of STS-7.

Sally brought Swarthmore and Stanford banners with her on STS-7.

TOUCHING DOWN

I started to feel heavier and heavier as gravity slowly pulled me into my seat. It was hard to lift my hand or hold my head up. Outside the windows the shuttle was engulfed in a fiery orange glow as we blazed through the air.

Bad weather forced the shuttle to land at Edwards Air Force Base in California instead of at the Kennedy Space Center in Florida. The shuttle made two extra orbits to get into position. When *Challenger* touched down on the desert runway, tens of thousands of people, including Sally's mother, father, and sister, cheered from Florida as they watched the landing on TV.

Commander Bob Crippen, Norm Thagard, and TFNG space rookies John Fabian, pilot Rick Hauck, and Sally brief the press after landing. They circled the earth for six days, making ninety-six orbits and covering 2.5 million miles.

After collecting stamps since her childhood, Sally could hardly believe that her own picture adorned one.

Once Sally's feet were back on the ground, her life changed forever. She was one of the most famous people on Earth. When Sally was a little girl, she collected stamps. Now Sally was on a stamp! She couldn't believe it.

Sally was invited to all sorts of events in her honor. Ballrooms were packed with politicians, celebrities, business executives, scientists, and education leaders. Everyone wanted to meet Sally and talk to her. Sometimes Sally's parents would come. Joyce saw how much it took out of her daughter to be the center of attention. At one banquet, after many hours and hundreds of handshakes, Sally told her mother, "I don't think I'll ever smile again."

Crew photo from Sally's *Challenger* flight, signed by Sally and mailed from the Kennedy Space Center.

Sally and crew at the White House with President Ronald Reagan.

Sally stands between women's sports advocate and tennis great Billie Jean King and women's rights advocate and respected journalist Gloria Steinem.

Everywhere Sally went, people recognized her. Everyone wanted to talk to her, shake her hand, and get her autograph. They wanted a photograph taken standing next to her. They wanted her to come to their child's school and talk to the students. They wanted her to come to their company and talk to their colleagues.

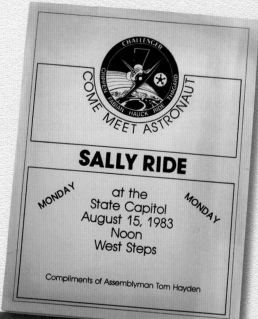

A flyer inviting the public to "come meet astronaut Sally Ride."

CHALLENGER

COME MEET ASTRONAUT

CRIPPEN FABIAN HAUCK RIDE THAGARD

SALLY RIDE

MONDAY at the State Capitol August 15, 1983 Noon West Steps MONDAY

Compliments of Assemblyman Tom Hayden

Sally at the podium at an event hosted by the Girls Club of America.

Sally tried her best to do it all. She was honored to be America's first woman in space. She felt a responsibility to NASA and to her country to share her experiences in space. But all the attention focused on her took a toll on Sally. She started feeling anxious and unhappy. Sally wasn't used to feeling that way.

Later that year, Molly Tyson threw a party for Sally in Palo Alto. Sally and Molly had stayed friends over the years, even though they seldom saw each other. Lots of people came to the party—some that Sally knew and others she'd never met. Everyone was having a good time. Everyone wanted to talk to Sally. When Ann Lebedeff finally got a chance to say hi to her, Sally said, "Let's go for a walk."

Ann and Sally walked and walked around the neighborhood. At first, Sally talked about how much fun she had in space. Then she confided in Ann that she was having a hard time with all of the attention she was getting. Sally told Ann, "I miss the days when no one knew who I was."

On *Sesame Street*.

Sally with Kathy Sullivan in front of NASA's *Challenger* space shuttle launch pad before their STS-41-G mission. During the mission, Kathy became the first woman to walk in space.

Some people like the attention that comes with being famous. Not Sally. Being a celebrity went against her basic nature. She was a quiet, private person—an introvert. Sally realized that she needed to talk to a professional about how she was feeling and figure out how to feel better. Sally saw a psychologist. The psychologist helped Sally understand her feelings. She helped Sally come up with ways to take better care of herself. Sally accepted fewer speeches, and she spent more time unwinding after giving talks and being in crowds.

When Sally returned to Houston, she started training for her second spaceflight. *Thank goodness. Back in training—safe again!* Sally thought to herself.

Sally's next flight would have a few "firsts," too:

First crew with two women: Sally and Kathy Sullivan
First woman to walk in space: Kathy

On October 5, 1984, *Challenger* lifted off from the Kennedy Space Center in Florida. During the eight-day mission, Sally and her crewmates used the robot arm to lift a 5,000-pound satellite out of the cargo bay. They gently pulled it away from the shuttle and then let go of it. Looking through a window, Sally watched the satellite fire its thrusters and then scoot away. It was packed with science instruments to study our planet. Over many years, it would measure Earth's ozone layer and the flow of heat from the warm tropics to the cooler poles.

Sally examines orbits with colleague Dave Leestma.

Bear and Dale with Bear's son, Whitney, in front of the launch site.

Sally put a 41-G crew patch on her flight notebook.

Sally was much more relaxed on her second spaceflight. She was an experienced astronaut! During the wake-up call from Mission Control on day two, Sally replied, "Hi. This is the 41-G crew. We're not in right now, but if you leave your name and number, we'll get right back to you." Sally's crewmates howled with laughter.

During the day three wake-up call, Sally answered, "I'm sorry, the number you've reached is not in service at this time. Please check the number and dial again, or contact your operator for assistance. Thank you for calling 41-G."

Sally's crewmates got into the fun, too. On day five, Marc Garneau, a Canadian astronaut, responded to the wake-up call in French with, "All lines are busy, please hold, and your call will be answered in the order it was received." And on day eight, Dave Leestma played part of the song "Rocket Man" by Elton John.

Luckily, the skies were clear in Florida on October 13, 1984. So Sally and her six crewmates landed back in Florida at the Kennedy Space Center.

Sally's accomplishments topped her wildest dreams. Yet deep down inside, she wasn't completely happy. There was a hole in Sally's heart that she needed to fill.

Sally kept a journal list of the space foods she liked and disliked.

Sally eating a meal while floating upside down inside the space shuttle.

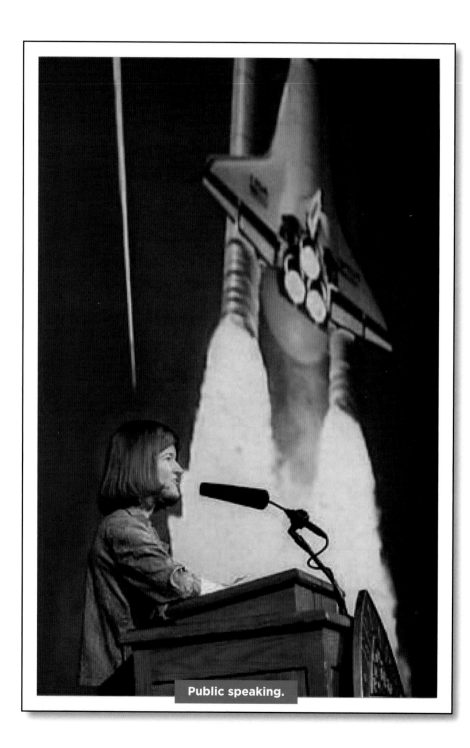

Public speaking.

5

That's the way to keep kids hooked on science!

As part of Sally's astronaut duties, she gave talks around the country. She showed her favorite photos looking back at Earth from space. She talked about what it's like to eat, sleep, and work in weightlessness. She laughed about doing somersaults in midair and floating grapes into the mouths of her crewmates.

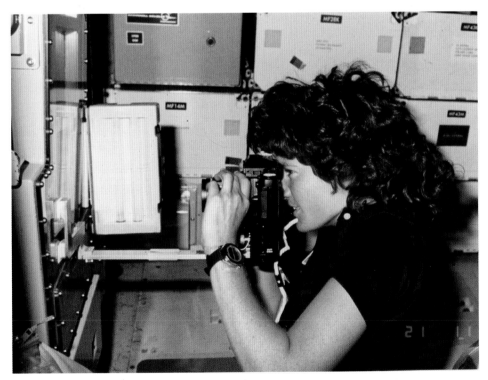

Sally taking photographs of a chemistry experiment during her first spaceflight.

Tam, after the 1986 Atlanta half-marathon. Sally trained for the race but fell ill and couldn't participate.

At the end of Sally's speeches, she always answered questions from students in the audience. This was her favorite part. "Young people ask the good questions that adults are afraid to ask," Sally said.

"Were you scared when you blasted off?"

"Yes! If you are not afraid, you don't understand what's about to happen to you."

"How do you go to the bathroom in space?"

"Carefully. The toilet has a long flexible tube with a removable cup at the end. Each astronaut has her or his own cup. To use the urine cup, you hold it next to your body while you are floating (yes, floating!) in the bathroom. The next step is very important! You turn on the air suction that flows through the hose. The air suction replaces gravity and pulls waste into a tank under the floor."

"When you eat floating upside down, is it hard to swallow your food?"

"No. Your body adjusts quickly to weightlessness. All of your body systems—your respiratory system, your digestive system, and so on—work the same as they do on Earth. So swallowing is easy."

When Sally was handed a list of speaking requests, she tried to pick cities where her friends lived. When Sally was heading to Washington, DC, she'd call Sue and they'd meet for lunch. When Sally was traveling to Atlanta, she'd call me and we'd get together for dinner or a movie.

Sally gave several talks in Atlanta. I was still living there and now teaching biology. Sometimes we would go for long walks and talk about science. Sally taught me about the universe and how it works. This made me look up more and wonder about distant galaxies. I taught Sally about living things and how they are connected to the rest of Earth. This made Sally look down more and wonder about the creatures she saw. Sally and I liked spending time together. Sally started coming to Atlanta every chance she got.

On one visit, in the spring of 1985, Sally and I took a long walk from my house to a nearby park. We stopped by the tennis courts and watched some kids taking a tennis lesson. Then we circled the lake and headed out of the park to a pizza parlor. Stuffed with salad and pizza, we strolled back to my house and plopped down on the couch. My cocker spaniel, Annie, had missed us, so I bent over to scrunch her ears. When I looked back at Sally . . . my heart skipped a beat. She was in love with me—and I was in love with her. What a sweet surprise! I had figured out that I was gay when I was twenty-two years old—and I was pretty comfortable with it. Fortunately, much of the fear that Sally felt about being gay was gone. Society was changing. It was becoming more accepting of people's differences. Sally was changing, too. She was becoming more accepting of herself.

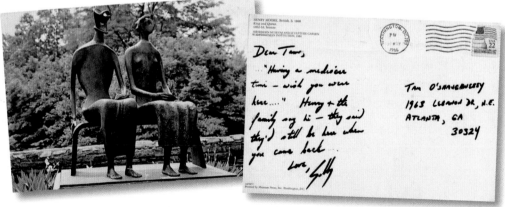

Sally sent Tam this card from one of their favorite art galleries, the Hirshhorn Museum and Sculpture Garden in Washington, DC.

Back home in Houston, Sally started training for her third shuttle mission. Then the unthinkable happened. On January 28, 1986, millions of TV viewers gasped in shock as the space shuttle *Challenger* exploded shortly after takeoff. All seven crewmembers were killed. They were Sally's friends. She was heartbroken.

Challenger's explosion made national headlines.

President Ronald Reagan asked Sally to be on the team that would investigate the tragedy. Over the coming months, the team learned that there had been signs of trouble on earlier *Challenger* flights, but they were ignored. One engineer, Roger Boisjoly, had even warned his bosses at the company that made the shuttle's rocket boosters and NASA that the boosters' seals, called O-rings, could weaken in cold weather. That's exactly what happened. *Challenger* lifted off on a very cold morning. Superheated rocket exhaust blew out through the seals and caused the shuttle to explode. After the investigation team heard Roger Boisjoly's testimony,

Sally gave him a hug. This was unusual for her. But Sally wanted him to know that she was proud of him for having the courage to tell the truth. The engineer's co-workers shunned him for telling the truth. But Sally never blindly followed the lead of other people. She kept an open mind and let the facts guide her conclusions.

The swearing-in ceremony for Sally and the other members of the Roger's Commission investigating the *Challenger* disaster.

Sally listens to evidence during the *Challenger* accident investigation.

Sally's retirement from NASA made headlines.

When the investigation ended, Sally realized that it would take NASA a long time to recover from the *Challenger* disaster. That meant it would be a long time before she could fly in space again. Sally decided not to wait. She retired from NASA.

Sally also decided to tell Steve that she no longer wanted to be married to him. Naturally, he was sad and upset. But Steve and Sally had started their relationship as good friends. They ended it the same way.

Sally had thought about what she wanted to do after leaving NASA and decided that she wanted to go back to the university life, but this time as a professor. She interviewed at the University of Georgia, Georgia Institute of Technology, and Emory University in Georgia, and at UCLA, Stanford

University, and UCSD in California. We talked things over. We both wanted to move back to California where we had grown up and where our parents and sisters lived. So Sally accepted a position as a physics professor at UCSD. I accepted a position teaching biology at San Diego Mesa College.

Then in the summer of 1989, Sally's father died unexpectedly after routine surgery. She was heartsick. She knew she would miss her daddy for the rest of her life.

Sally and Dale.

Sally began her new job at UCSD in the fall of 1989. When she picked up her teaching schedule, she got a big surprise. *Rats!* she thought. Sally's old nemesis Electricity and Magnetism would be the very first course she taught. As Sally prepared her lectures and homework assignments, she knew she had to change her attitude. She worked hard to write lectures with fascinating examples of electromagnetism to help her students understand it and to keep them (and herself!) interested.

Sally taught Electricity and Magnetism for two quarters. Then she taught other courses in physics. She also created a new course on space exploration for non-science majors. Her classes were very popular. Besides teaching, Sally mentored graduate students on their physics research and careers. She also teamed up with her students and other physics professors on articles that were published in physics journals.

I began my new teaching post that winter. While I was teaching biology in Atlanta and now in San Diego, I noticed that my students had a wide range of critical thinking and study skills. The better these skills, the better the understanding of science concepts. I talked with Sally about this. *Uhm, that's true for my students, too,* she said. I began to wonder about how people learn. In time, I studied school psychology for my Ph.D. at the University of California, Riverside, and became a professor in that field.

Sally reads a Dr. Seuss book aloud at a UCSD library event.

Sally and Tam with Gypsy.

Sally hugging Maggie.

A family portrait: Sally, Tam, niece Cait, nephew Whit, Bear, and Bear's partner, Susan Craig.

Hiking near the Pacific Ocean.

Sally and I loved to browse through bookstores. We would head straight for the science section, and then go by the science fiction and young adult sections. It bothered us that the young adult section had so few science books and that many of them were deadly dull . . . even if you liked science! Then one day I came across *Is There Life on Other Worlds?* by Isaac Asimov. As I skimmed the pages of the book, I grew more and more excited. I hurried to find Sally in the next aisle. "Look at this book!" I said.

Sally flipped through the pages and then said, "Wow. This is a very good book."

Isaac Asimov wrote beautifully, explained science concepts clearly, and had a good sense of humor. "That's the way to keep kids hooked on science," I said.

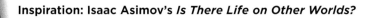

Inspiration: Isaac Asimov's *Is There Life on Other Worlds?*

After her second spaceflight, Sally co-wrote a book with Sue Okie about her adventures in space. Now Sally and I wanted to try our hands at writing science books for girls and boys that were as fun and fascinating as Isaac Asimov's. Our first was *Voyager: An Adventure to the Edge of the Solar System*, which described the journey of two spindly spacecrafts, *Voyager I* and *Voyager II*, across billions of miles of space to give scientists their first close-up look at the giant planets—Jupiter, Saturn, Uranus, and Neptune. On the notebook we used to record our research and notes for the book, we wrote our initials: TOS SKR. The acronym TOSKR became our private signature.

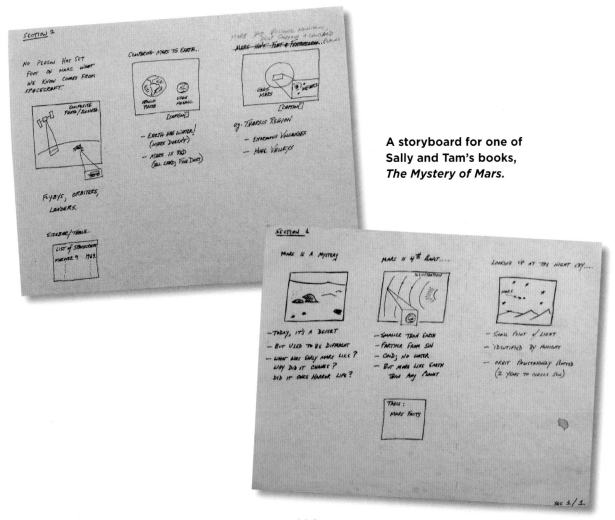

A storyboard for one of Sally and Tam's books, *The Mystery of Mars.*

Certificate naming a star in Orion "TOSKR," given by Sally to Tam for her birthday.

A few years later, on my birthday, Sally surprised me with a very unusual present: a star! Sally found out how to have a star in the Orion constellation named TOSKR.

Sally and I continued to write together—on top of our work as university professors. Over the next several years, we wrote books about exploring Mars and the rest of our solar system, with robotic spacecraft that act like scientists' eyes, ears, and noses. We also wrote about exploring our own planet, and how the broader view from space lets scientists study the bigger patterns of Earth's air, oceans, lands, and life.

Sally and Tam liked to sit across from each other at their dining room table to write their books.

Sally and Tam giving a talk together in 2009.

One idea for a book kept swirling around in our minds—Earth's changing climate. The topic was on the front page of the newspaper and on the nightly news—Earth's air is getting warmer; Arctic sea ice is melting; sea levels are rising; and animals from pikas to polar bears are searching for cooler habitats.

Sally and I knew that we would have to learn a lot about a lot of topics to write this book. So we dug in. We read the latest research, and we talked to experts. We made an outline and a storyboard. Then we divvied up the parts of the outline and started writing. We wrote and rewrote. Sally and I read aloud to each other and gave each other feedback. After nearly two years, we finished the book. "Shweeww," sighed Sally. "I don't think I'll ever write again!"

Sally and Tam's second book, *The Third Planet*.

Mission Planet Earth.

Wherever Sally traveled to give a talk, she met students, parents, and teachers who were fascinated by space. Talking about this with her colleagues, she came up with an idea to put a camera on the space shuttle that students could control from their classrooms. "It gives young people the gee-whiz wonder of space and real hands-on science," she said.

Sally took the lead. She persuaded NASA to put a digital camera on the space shuttle and to fund the project. She convinced UCSD to give her office space on campus to build an EarthKAM Mission Control like the one at Johnson Space Center in Houston. In 1995, EarthKAM was launched. Since then, hundreds of thousands of students from around the world have used the EarthKAM camera, which is now on the space station. They've snapped nearly 100,000 images. They've studied everything from deforestation in the Amazon and dust storms in Africa to volcanoes in Hawaii and phytoplankton in the Indian Ocean.

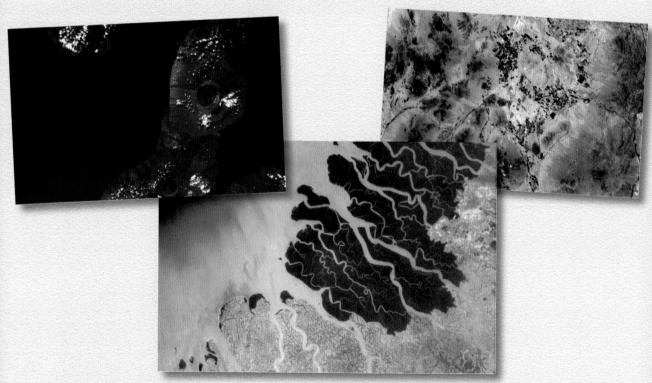

Images taken by students using EarthKAM: (left to right) the Galápagos Islands; the Ganges River Delta, India; and the Arizona desert.

Through teaching, writing, speaking, and projects such as EarthKAM, Sally and I became more and more involved in keeping girls and boys interested in science. We'd heard that many young people—especially girls and minority students—abandon their early interests in science as they go through school. *Why?* we wondered.

Studies on girls' and boys' science interests, achievements, attitudes, and beliefs show that the reason why young people drift away from science is not because they don't like it or aren't good at it. It's because our society sends false messages about who scientists are, what they do, and how they work. Television, magazines, movies, newspapers, and even science textbooks, too, often portray science as dull and difficult and not very cool—and show scientists as nerds who work alone wearing lab coats, pocket protectors, and thick glasses. *No wonder!* we thought.

With this in mind, we met with three friends from UCSD: Karen Flammer, Terry McEntee, and Alann Lopes. Sally sprang the idea: "Let's start a company!" Ever since she was a kid, Sally liked to play team sports better than she liked to play individual sports. Even in tennis, she liked playing doubles better than singles. It was no different now. Sally preferred working with a team of people rather than working alone.

In 2001, we started the company and named it Sally Ride Science. Our goal was to bring science to life through science events and books. We wanted to show young people (and their parents and teachers!) that science is fascinating, creative, and fun; and that the women and men working in science are regular people who come from all walks of life. Sally had never liked the attention that fame brought. But for the first time in her life, Sally was happy to use her fame. It was for a good cause—it was for something she believed in passionately. "Everywhere I go I meet girls and boys who want to be astronauts and explore space," she said. "Or they love the ocean and want to be oceanographers, or they love animals and want to be zoologists, or they love designing things and want to be engineers. I want to see those same stars in their eyes in ten years, and know they are on their way!"

Speaking with children during a book signing at a Sally Ride Science Festival.

Giving a keynote speech at a Sally Ride Science Festival.

We threw ourselves into our work. Sally was head of the company and raised money from friends and colleagues to get the business going. It wasn't very long, though, before Sally Ride Science was standing on its own financial feet! Karen would run the EarthKAM program and eventually teacher training, too. Alann would be responsible for technology. Terry would organize science festivals, together with Sally's sister Bear. And I would be head of content—for our website, teacher training, and books— and eventually help Sally run the company.

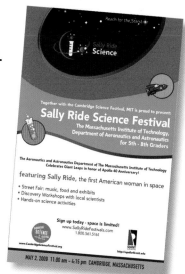

A poster advertising a Sally Ride Science Festival.

Sally had her fingers in everything—from forming partnerships with other companies and science museums to brainstorming the look and feel of the website; and from coming up with ideas for science books to calling engineers around the country to be judges for our national toy design competition. She liked to walk around the office—on her toes, of course. She'd drop by someone's office and ask them what they were working on, throw out ideas, and tell funny stories. She inspired everyone because she worked so hard, had high expectations of everyone, and always kept her sense of humor. Sally brought out the best in people.

Still, starting a company isn't an easy thing to do. Sally and the rest of us hardly had any experience! We learned along the way—how to run science festivals for thousands of students, how to convince corporate America to back us, and how to publish science books. We worked hard. We had fun!

Sally and I and our three friends dreamed of building a business that would do good things—and make a difference. That's just what we did. Over the next twelve years, Sally Ride Science grew from a staff of five to fifty. We ran a hundred science festivals around the country. We published a monthly science newsletter and ninety science and science career books. We trained thousands of teachers on how to spark and sustain interest in science, and reached millions of students with our books and events.

A Sally Ride Science Teacher Training Binder.

A postcard announcing the Sally Ride Science documentary film, *Some Assembly Required*, which followed five teams during the 2008 year-long TOYchallenge competition.

Sally's official photo as CEO of Sally Ride Science.

Sally talking with teachers at a Sally Ride Science Academy.

Away from teaching, traveling, and running the company, Sally and I liked a quiet home life. We walked our two dogs, Gypsy and Maggie. Sometimes we played darts or Ping-Pong, or chess or Scrabble. Sally had the edge in Scrabble and darts. I had the edge in chess and Ping-Pong. On weekends, we saw our friends or walked in Torrey Pines State Park. Sometimes we played tennis and laughed about how horrible we were now. And we talked about the company—how to reach more teachers and students, what science concepts to cover in our next books, when to redo our website . . . and on and on. We couldn't help ourselves.

One hot summer day, Sally and I were reading the newspaper in the living room, with the doors open to the backyard to let in a breeze. All of a sudden a mourning dove was walking around by the couch! We tried to coax the dove back outside, but it got scared and started flying around the living room. The dove tried to fly through a window above a high ledge, again and again. It became exhausted from trying and just sat on the ledge in shock.

Sally and I quickly figured out what to do. We would get the tall ladder from the garage. I am afraid of heights, so Sally would climb the ladder. Sally was afraid of touching the dove, so I showed her how to hold it. Sally slowly climbed the ladder and gently grasped the dove with both hands. Sally was ten feet off the ground, so I stood on a chair, reached up, and carefully took the dove from her. I stepped off the chair and walked through the open doors onto the grass. When I opened my hands, the dove flew away. "Let's never do that again!" Sally said.

A few of Sally's many photographs of mourning doves.

Sally was thrilled to carry the Olympic flame during the 2002 Salt Lake City Olympic Torch Relay in San Diego, California. She loved the Olympics and collected stamps of Olympic sports, athletes, and host cities since early childhood.

Some of Sally's habits:

She . . .
walked and ran on her toes.
clicked her tongue to music (instead of humming or singing).
ate popcorn soaked in milk with a spoon.
ate watermelon sprinkled in salt.
never ripped the top off of a sugar or tea packet (it might float away!).
woke up happy almost every day.
lived in the moment—seldom thought about the past or the future.

Sally and I had known each other since we were girls. Our friendship was like threads of gold running through our lives. We had each other, we had a booming business, we had wonderful friends and families. Then in an instant, everything changed.

In March 2011, a large crew from Sally Ride Science attended the National Science Teachers Association conference in San Francisco. Sally Ride Science was hosting a party to launch our new science book series. On the taxi ride over to the party, Sally told me that she didn't feel very well. I noticed that her cheeks were slightly yellow. Sally made the announcement about the new books at the party. The next morning, we flew back to San Diego. We drove straight from the airport to the doctor's office. After a physical exam and some tests, Sally's doctor looked at her with tears in his eyes. He said, "Sally, you have a tumor in your pancreas. I'm so sorry, but you have pancreatic cancer."

We couldn't believe our ears. For the next few weeks, we saw doctor after doctor. Sally had test after test. We tried to make sense of what was happening to us. We talked and talked. We cried and cried. Then we did what we always did—we learned everything we could about pancreatic cancer—from its symptoms and causes to its diagnoses and treatments. Sally and I studied pancreatic cancer to learn how to fight it.

We found out that eating vegan (no red meat or dairy; lots of fruits, vegetables, nuts, and beans) might slow Sally's cancer and might prevent diseases like cancer in me. So we became vegans. We learned that meditation is a scientifically proven way to relax. So we started meditating every day. Sally wanted to be as fit as possible for surgery and set up yoga lessons at home. The lessons didn't last long though. The yoga instructor showed us how to do each of the moves in the Sun Salutation. Then she passed out a sheet of paper with an Indian chant typed on it. She began chanting really loud, "ong namo guru dev namo," in a beautiful voice that filled the room. But Sally and I barely whispered the words. We didn't dare look at each other for fear of bursting out laughing. Sally took the next lesson by herself. She didn't schedule any others.

In the meantime, Sally's doctors came up with a game plan to tackle the cancer. Sally would have chemotherapy followed by radiation. This would slow the growth of the cancer and kill the cancer cells around the edges of the tumor. Then Sally would have surgery to get rid of the tumor. After Sally recovered from surgery, she would go through another round of chemotherapy and radiation to kill any cancer cells that might survive.

All her life Sally had been intensely private. The people she admired— her heroes—also tended to be private people: her teacher Dr. Elizabeth Mommaerts, aviator Amelia Earhart, pitching great Sandy Koufax, astronaut Neil Armstrong. When Sally was an astronaut, she learned the hard way that being famous comes with a price tag. So she told me that she only wanted a small group of family and friends to know she had cancer. Sally wanted us to focus our time and energy on her getting well—not dealing with the press.

The staff at Sally Ride Science—taken in honor of Sally's birthday.

Tam and Karen Flammer celebrate Sally's birthday.

Every Tuesday at noon, Karen and Terry, our friends from Sally Ride Science, came over to the house with lunch. They usually brought Sally's favorite Greek food—hummus with pita bread and horiatiki salad with warm lentil pilaf. We called the visits "founder's lunches." But Terry and Karen just wanted to spend time with Sally.

Sally started feeling better. Everyone had high hopes that she would be okay. Then we learned that Sally's cancer had spread. Sally and I knew we didn't have much time. We talked about our life together. Bear came to visit and help out as often as she could. Sally's mother, Joyce, her niece Cait, and nephew Whit came, too. We all wished we had more time together.

Sally would usually hear me coming up the stairs or feel me sitting down on the edge of the bed. With her eyes half closed, Sally would smile. It was not just a slight smile that turned up the corners of her lips; it was a great big smile that took over her whole face. One morning she looked at me and said, "I know you know how much I love you. But I want to make sure you know how much everything we have had together and everything we have done together—all of these years—means to me."

"I know," I whispered. Tears welled up in both of our eyes. We hugged each other like we never wanted to let go.

A Ride family holiday gathering.

Sally with nephew Whit and niece Cait.

Sally could hardly believe she'd actually made it into space.

A few days later, Sally closed her eyes and drifted into a coma.
10:10 a.m., Monday, July 23, 2012.
Like a warm whisper, Sally took her last breath of air. Sally left behind a better world because she . . .

thought for herself.

was true to herself.

broke gender barriers with her skill, confidence, hard work, and humor.

inspired girls and boys to be themselves, to be courageous, and to reach for their dreams.

Next time you see Orion twinkling on a clear dark night or hear a mourning dove cooing on a warm summer day, think of Sally. If she could, she would borrow the last line of our favorite poem, Mary Oliver's "The Summer Day," and say to you . . .

"Tell me, what is it you plan to do with your one wild and precious life?"

One of Sally's favorite photographs: Earth and the moon from the shuttle.

CAST OF CHARACTERS

JOYCE RIDE, mother

Joyce continues to visit and counsel women in prison. And she continues to use her sharp wit to entertain her friends and family.

DALE RIDE, father

Deceased

KAREN "BEAR" RIDE, sister

Bear is still the director of Sally Ride Science Festivals and very involved in the Presbyterian Church. Her two kids, Cait and Whit, now have families of their own. Bear is married to Susan Craig.

ANDERS ANDERSON (Grandpa Andy), maternal grandfather

Deceased

ADA SULEM ANDERSON (Grandma Ada), maternal grandmother

Deceased

WHITNEY GRANT, friend

After a successful career training horses, Whitney now trains dogs on her ranch near Santa Inez, California.

ANN LEBEDEFF, friend

Ann is a professor of physical education and an award-winning women's tennis coach at Pomona College in Southern California.

TAM O'SHAUGHNESSY, life and business partner

I am now the chief executive officer of Sally Ride Science. Our company continues to run EarthKAM, train teachers, and create science books and science career books—now eBooks. I still hike in Torrey Pines State Park. And I am still careful not to leave the living room doors open in the summer.

SUE OKIE, friend

After a successful career as a physician and medical reporter for the *Washington Post*, Sue now writes poetry. She is married to Walter Weiss. They have two sons, Peter and Jacob.

DR. ELIZABETH MOMMAERTS, eleventh grade science teacher

Deceased

MOLLY TYSON, college roommate

After a successful career as a technical writer at Apple, Molly now teaches English as a second language to immigrants in San Francisco.

STEVE HAWLEY, former husband

Steve flew on five space shuttle missions. He is retired from NASA and is now a professor of physics and astronomy at the University of Kansas, Lawrence. He is married to Eileen Keegan.

TIMELINE OF SALLY RIDE'S LIFE

1951

Born on May 26 in Los Angeles, California

1956–1957

Goes to kindergarden and first grade at Hayvenhurst Elementary School

1958–1959

Goes to second and third grades at Gault Street Elementary School

1960

Spends a year in Europe with her family (Sally misses fourth grade.)

1961

Goes to sixth grade at Encino Elementary School (Sally skips fifth grade because she is ahead of her age group in reading and math.)

1962–1964

Goes to seventh through ninth grades at Gaspar de Portola Junior High School

1965–1968

Goes to tenth through twelfth grades at Westlake School for Girls in Los Angeles, California

1968

Graduates from Westlake School for Girls

Starts freshman year at Swarthmore College

1970

Takes summer classes at UCLA

Starts junior year at Stanford University

1973

Receives bachelor's degrees in physics and English from Stanford University

1975

Receives master's degree in physics from Stanford University

1977

Applies to become an astronaut when NASA conducts a national search for new astronauts and, for the first time, allows women to apply

1978

Receives Ph.D. degree in physics from Stanford University

Selected by NASA as an astronaut candidate—one of six women among thirty-five trainees chosen

1978–1982

Astronaut training

Flying in T-38 jets

Parachute jumping and water survival courses

Develops shuttle's robot arm

Serves as communications officer (CAPCOM) for STS-2 and STS-3 missions, communicating with shuttle crews from Mission Control

1983

On June 18, becomes the first American woman to fly in space

Serves as mission specialist on STS-7 aboard space shuttle *Challenger*

1984

On October 5, flies on second space shuttle mission

Serves as mission specialist on STS-41-G, also aboard *Challenger*

1985

Assigned to crew of third space shuttle flight, STS-61-M

1986

Mission training suspended in January after the space shuttle *Challenger* explodes shortly after launch

Appointed to the presidential commission investigating the *Challenger* disaster

1987

Assigned to NASA headquarters in Washington, DC

Creates NASA's Office of Exploration for long-range planning

Produces a widely acclaimed report, "Leadership and America's Future in Space"

Retires from NASA

Becomes a science fellow at the Center for International Security and Arms Control at Stanford University

1988

Inducted into the National Women's Hall of Fame

1989

Becomes professor of physics and director of the California Space Institute at the University of California, San Diego (UCSD)

1994

Creates EarthKAM, an ongoing NASA program that involves middle school students in selecting, shooting, downloading, and studying photos of Earth from cameras aboard the International Space Station

1995

Wins prestigious American Institute of Physics Children's Science Writing Award with co-author Tam O'Shaughnessy for *The Third Planet: Exploring the Earth from Space*

2001

Co-founds a science education company, Sally Ride Science, to inspire girls and boys to stick with their interests in science and to consider careers in science, technology, engineering, and math (STEM)

2003

Named to NASA's Accident Investigation Board to investigate the cause of the space shuttle *Columbia* disaster

Inducted into the Astronaut Hall of Fame at the Kennedy Space Center

2005

Awarded the NCAA's Theodore Roosevelt "Teddy" Award, the highest honor presented to a former student-athlete

2006

Inducted into the California Hall of Fame

2007

Inducted into the National Aviation Hall of Fame

Retired early from UCSD to devote her time and energy to Sally Ride Science; named emeritus professor of physics.

2009

Named one of America's Best Leaders by *U.S. News & World Report*

2010

Co-founded and served on the board of Change the Equation, a national nonprofit initiative led by top corporate executives to improve education in science, technology, engineering, and math

2012

Awarded the 2012 National Space Grant Distinguished Service Award

Continued to serve as CEO of Sally Ride Science and to encourage young people across the country to pursue their interests in science until her death on July 23, 2012

2013

Posthumously awarded the Presidential Medal of Freedom, the nation's highest civilian honor

Honored by NASA renaming of EarthKAM to Sally Ride EarthKAM

Received the Space Foundation's General James E. Hill Lifetime Space Achievement Award

Named a Stanford University Engineering Hero

2014

U.S. Navy names research vessel, R/V *Sally Ride* (AGOR); it will be operated by Scripps Institution of Oceanography at UCSD in La Jolla

Tam O'Shaughnessy and Sally Ride on October 16, 2010.

Tam accepts the Presidential Medal of Freedom on Sally's behalf at the White House on November 20, 2013.

Painting created for the national tribute to Sally, held at the John F. Kennedy Center in Washington, DC, on May 20, 2013.

Christening Ceremony
SALLY RIDE
AGOR 28 Hull 59
Sponsor: Tam E. O'Shaughnessy, Ph.D.
Builder: Dakota Creek Industries, Inc.
Anacortes, Washington

Tam christens the navy's new research vessel *Sally Ride* on August 9, 2014. It is the first research ship to be named after a woman.

INDEX

ACKNOWLEDGMENTS

This book is based on my memories of Sally—from the summer of 1964 to the summer of 2012. It is also based on the many photographs, papers, and mementos Sally saved throughout her life. I am thankful to Sally's mother, Joyce, and her sister, Bear, for retelling the family stories to me—one more time—especially the ones about Sally's early childhood and the trip to Europe. Thanks also to Bear for helping me locate and identify photographs of Sally when she was very young. And, thanks to Sue Okie for sharing her stories of Sally at Westlake and Swarthmore in the late 1960s, to Molly Tyson for sharing her recollections and photographs of Sally at Stanford in the early 1970s, and to Ann Lebedeff for sharing her reminiscences and pictures of Sally from the mid 1970s and from Sally's first space shuttle launch in June 1983.

I am very grateful to my friends—Betsy Butler, Kay Loveland, Billie Jean King, and Twyla Tharp—for helping me find the confidence and courage to write this book. Although I've written a dozen science books for young adults and conceived and edited dozens more, this was my first biography—and its subject matter extremely personal and precious to me. Finally, many thanks to Betsy, Kay, Twyla, and Billie Jean for their insightful comments on various stages of the manuscript; and to my longtime editor, Simon Boughton, for his extraordinary skill and wise counsel throughout the creation of this book.

PHOTO CREDITS

American Library Association: p. 131, top; Ann Lebedoff: p. 57, all; p. 58; AP Photo/Dave Pickoff: p. 113, left; AP Photo/NASA/Carla Cioffi/REX: p. 151, center; AP Photo/PKS: p. 123, bottom; AP/Photo/Richard Drew: p. 110, bottom; p. 111, bottom; AP Photo/Scott Stewart: p. 110, top; p. 123, top; Ari Hauben: p. 151, top; © Bettmann/CORBIS: opening page; p. 87, bottom; Chuck Painter/Stanford News Service: p. 81; Eric Long, Smithsonian National Air and Space Museum: p. 40, top (NASM 2015-01304); p. 43 (NASM 2015-01305); p. 34 (NASM 2015-01306); p. 13, top (NASM 2015-01307); p. 107, bottom right (NASM 2015-01308); Geni Lebedoff: p. 101; Harvard-Westlake School: p. 46, bottom; p. 47, top; p. 48; p. 49, all; John Oxley Library, State Library of Queensland: p. 30, top; Karen "Bear" Ride: p. 90, all; p. 99, top left & right; Kay Loveland: p. 127, top left; Molly Tyson: p. 67; p. 68; p. 71; p. 73, top; p. 75; NASA: opening page; p. 84; p. 86; p. 87, top; p. 91, bottom; p. 92, all; p. 93, all; p. 94; p. 95; p. 98, all; p. 100, top; p. 104; p. 105; p. 106, all; p. 107, shuttle; p. 108; p. 109, bottom; p. 113, right; p. 114; p. 117; p. 119; p. 144; p. 145; Rebecca Lawson Photography: p. 136, top; Courtesy of the Ride Family: p. 2; p. 3; p. 4; p. 5, all; p. 6; p. 7, all; p. 8; p. 9, all; p. 10; p. 11, top; p. 12; p. 15; p. 16; p. 17; p. 18; p. 19; p. 20; p. 21, all; p. 22, all; p. 23; p. 24; p. 25, all; p. 26; p. 27; p. 31, all; p. 32; p. 35; p. 36; p. 37; p. 47, center & bottom; p. 62; p. 65, bottom; p. 102, all; p. 103, all; p. 115, top; Sally Ride Science: p. 118, p. 132, all; p. 134, all; p. 135, all; p. 136, bottom; p. 141; Courtesy of Tam O'Shaughnessy: p. 11, bottom; p. 13, bottom left & right; p. 14, all; p. 28, all; p. 29, all; p. 30, bottom; p. 39; p 40, bottom; p. 41; p. 42; p. 44; p. 45; p. 46, top; p. 47, top right; p. 50; p. 51; p. 52; p. 53, all; p. 54; p. 56, p. 59, bottom; p. 60, all; p. 61, all; p. 63; p. 64 all; pg. 65, top; p. 66; p. 70; p. 73, bottom; p. 74; p. 76; p. 77; p. 78, all; p. 79, all; p. 80, all; p. 83, all; p. 85, all; p. 88, all; p. 89, all; p. 91, top right; p. 96; p. 97, all; p. 99, bottom; p. 100, bottom; p. 107, bottom left; p. 109, top; p. 111, top; p. 115, bottom; p. 116; p. 120; p. 121; p. 122; p. 124; p. 125; p. 126; p. 127, top right & bottom; p. 128, all; p. 129, all; p. 130; p. 131, center & bottom; p. 138, all; p. 142; p. 143, all; Todd Warshaw/Getty: p. 139; U.S. Navy Photo by John F. Williams: p. 151, bottom; USTA: p. 59, top; Vicki Fletcher: p. 150